THE
TWILIGHT
OF
CITIES

Water drops have worn the stones of Troy,
And blind oblivion swallow'd cities up,
And mighty states characterless are grated
To dusty nothing.

—*Troilus and Cressida*

THE
TWILIGHT
OF
CITIES

E. A. GUTKIND

New York: The Free Press of Glencoe

London: Macmillan   New York

THIS book is dedicated to
the critics who are willing to listen
and to the consenters who are
willing to act.

PREFACE

This is a new book by a partially revised author, although it is based on some of my previous works. In the first part, "Cities of 180 Generations," I have made use of sections of the chapter "Streets and Houses," which appeared in my *Revolution of Environment*, and in general a certain affinity exists with my *Expanding Environment*. However, the ideas and suggestions contained in my other publications have been considerably elaborated with many new reflections and viewpoints.

The number of footnotes is reduced to a minimum. I wanted to make this book readable not only for professional experts but, above all, for the general public. In any case, complete acknowledgment of sources is impossible in a book of this kind; but I wish to express in a general though no less sincere manner my great obligation to all those writers without whose invaluable contributions this work could not have been written.

Similar considerations have convinced me that a bibliography should not be added, but I would refer readers to the very comprehensive bibliographies contained in all volumes of my forthcoming *International History of City Development.*

My thanks are due to Mr. R. Maxwell, A.R.I.B.A., and to Mr. Ahmed El Naggar.

E.A.G.

University of Pennsylvania,
Philadelphia
August, 1962

CONTENTS

THE
TWILIGHT
OF
CITIES

chapter one

CITIES OF 180
GENERATIONS

THIS historical survey is of necessity condensed and simplified. It intends to describe and interpret the transformation of the physical layout of cities as the symbolic expression of the ever-renewed religious, social, political, and economic ideas that have revolutionized man's environment. Without a knowledge of the development of cities in the past it is difficult to evaluate urban life in the present and chart a course for future action. The survey shows how intimately the structure of settlement has been related to the general ideas of a period, and how greatly the springs of action have been influenced by this mutual dependence.

About 180 generations separate us from the first cities.

An uninterrupted line of development runs from the earliest cities of Sumer and the Indus Valley to the present time. The function, size, and structure of cities have changed in detail during these five thousand years, but the general features which distinguished urban from rural life have remained basically the same. The cities created a type of human being whose mental attitude divorced him from the peasants and their ways of living.

The intimate solidarity with Nature was cut and a new type of man was born when the Urban Revolution completed the work that the Agricultural Revolution had begun. These two revolutions laid the foundation on which our present civilization rests. It is not correct to assume that the Urban Revolution had a less profound impact upon the transformation of the environment than the Agricultural Revolution, that its main achievements were social and economic innovations, and that the basis of subsistence was not fundamentally altered. This easy simplification does not do justice to the relative importance of each of the two revolutions.

True, the development of agriculture affected larger areas and was more conspicuous in changing the face of the earth, at least during the earlier periods. It had profound social and economic consequences for the people who carried it through. It transformed them from migrant hunters and food-gatherers into sedentary groups with different social and economic habits and aspirations—a change that was by no means less remarkable than the transition from rural to urban existence.

The two revolutions were interacting. Cities could not come into being before agriculture could produce a food surplus to support the city dwellers, who were engaged in nonagricultural activities. Rural communities could not expand or increase their food production without a growing number of consumers, or without the benefit of interchange of their products for goods manufactured in the cities, although this exchange was at the beginning only a minor part of the mutual dependence.

ANCIENT CITIES

Mesopotamia.   All higher civilizations, with the possible exception of the Mayan, have created cities at a relatively early stage of their existence. The first cities came into being in Mesopotamia, along the Tigris and Euphrates rivers or in their immediate neighborhood. Our knowledge of urban development during the early centuries is still very scanty. Archeological evidence is incomplete, and data on the life of the common people and their residential districts are too sporadic to provide sufficient information on the initial period of urbanization. We may, however, make certain deductions from the little we know from written records and the available archeological evidence.

It would seem that more than two millennia elapsed before the village communities had sufficiently increased in size and consolidated their internal structure to grow into the city-states of Sumer. This happened toward the end of the fourth millenium B.C., when the village communities had spread from the mountainous areas down into the river valleys. Gradually a complex and stratified social and economic structure developed that regulated the life and work of the citizenry and influenced with increasing intensity their mode of thinking.

Irrigation, first on a small scale, individual and sporadic, and later organized on a large scale, improved the productivity of agriculture and strengthened the need for cooperation. However, controlled irrigation was more a concomitant than an actual cause of city development. The cities had to reach a certain degree of internal consolidation before they could exert a constructive influence on the organization of collective irrigation. But once this stage was reached, urbanization and irrigation control moved in the same direction and became more and more interdependent.

The cities grew into centers of organization and distribution, and of technical and economic progress until, between 3000 and 2500 B.C., the fully developed city-states had finally taken root. It is most likely that the temple preceded the palace as the centralizing power, and that with this process the stratification of society increased and its technological advance continued.

Unfortunately, we have hardly any knowledge of the physical layout of the cities of Mesopotamia, except as regards walls and temples. How the common people lived, what their quarters looked like and how they were laid out, we do not know. We might perhaps assume that the residential quarters were densely built up without any apparent system and that they looked not too different from those of present-day oriental towns such as Erbil. The residential districts were grouped around the public buildings, which occupied the central area. This part of the city was laid out more regularly, with wide streets crossing one another at right angles. The rest of the city was a chaotic mass of dwellings, crowded together in a relatively small area, and traversed by winding, narrow unpaved lanes. The main roads led from the center to the gates in the walls. Some of the more important cities in the lower river valleys covered an area of more than 250 acres—Uruk more than 1,100 acres, with a population of about 50,000 inhabitants.

Trade, apart from the sufficient supply of food and raw materials, was another factor which contributed to the growth of urbanization. It extended as far as the Indus Valley and Syria. Later the cities of Mesopotamia may have been entrepôts for the trade with Asia. Here converged later the caravan routes leading to what are now Merv, Bukhara, Samarkand, Kashgar, and further to China, and from Merv possibly southward to Baktra, Kabul, and through the Khyber Pass to India. In Nahum (3.16) we read about Nineveh: "Thou hast multiplied thy merchants above the stars of heaven." The cities included large open spaces that were used as fields, gardens, and orchards, contributing to the food supply of the population.

Indus Valley.   The cities of the Indus Valley, Mohenjo-Daro and Harappa, date back to the third millennium B.C. Excavations have revealed a highly developed culture and the existence of an urban society based on agriculture and trade. The civilization was apparently centralized, like the contemporary civilizations of Egypt and Sumer. The two cities are separated from each other by a distance of about four hundred miles. It is still an unresolved question whether they were united under one rule or had separate governments.

Each was dominated by a citadel, situated not at the center but on one side of the urban area near the walls. The outline of each city is roughly a parallelogram of about 400 by 200 yards, its main axis running north to south. On the lower ground, near the citadel, stood blocks of barracks or coolie-quarters and storehouses, marshaled, as Sir Mortimer

Wheeler says, like a military cantonment, and bespeaking authority. It may be assumed that the administration of the rulers of these cities resembled that of the priest-kings of Sumer and Akkad and that the social structure was not too dissimilar to that of the other great riparian civilizations.

Egypt.   Urbanization and trade in Egypt were on the whole less pronounced than in Mesopotamia, with the exception of trade in the Delta. Settlements developed around temples, palaces, and tombs. Trade and industry were secondary in importance, although the quality of production was extremely high. Agriculture was the main pursuit. It is not unlikely that as early as the middle of the fourth millennium B.C. some villages grew into central places as the capitals of the *nomes,* the clan divisions, exerting at the same time a certain protective function for their territory.

Here the local feudal lords may have erected a temple and other public buildings and tried to promote handicraft and to secure a regular supply of agricultural products. These places acted as a sort of market for the district and possessed granaries. Roads, as everywhere, were important factors in the development of towns. Only in the later periods did the character of cities become more distinct.

In earlier times the significance of a city was dependent on the duration of the reign of the Pharaoh, or the dynasty. The building of a new capital at the accession to the throne of a new ruler is nothing unusual. We find it also in other parts of Africa. Livingstone reports, for instance, that the last seven kings of the Kazembe built seven new residences within a distance of only a few miles. Temples have always been centers of administration and treasure houses accumulating wealth in goods and land. Breasted reports in the *History of Egypt:*

The records of Ramses III for the first and only time in Egyptian history enable us to determine the total amount of property owned and controlled by the temples. An inventory in the Papyrus Harris covering almost all the temples of the country shows that they possessed over 107,000 slaves. The temples thus owned 2 per cent of the population. In land we find the sacred endowments amounting to nearly three-quarters of a million acres, that is, nearly one-seventh, or over 14½ per cent of the cultivable land of the country; and as some of the smaller temples like that of Khnum are omitted in the inventory it is safe to say that the total holdings of the temples amounted to 15 per cent of the available land in the country.

In general the temple economy was more concerned with accumulating and administering wealth than with the promotion of its uninterrupted circulation.

India.   The old towns of India were limited in size. They reflected the ground plan of the world as devised by the Jainas, a religious group of North India related to the Buddhists. The innermost circle is occupied by the Earth, which is surrounded by a circular ocean. In the center rises Meru, the world mountain, from which issue four rivers separating four continents. Beyond the circular ocean is another circular continent with its mountain, followed by another ocean and another continent. The bounding of the town by a wall, the situation of the temple or the palace in the center, the principle of walled-in quarters, the symbolism of figures, as seen, for instance, in the number of gates (twelve gates corresponding to the twelve signs of the Zodiac), the symbolism of colors—all these factors were a direct transposition of the world concept into architecture, even though the cities were mostly rectangular, and only very occasionally, as in the case of the old town of Crikshatra in Burma, circular.

According to old Indian ideas, cosmic forces govern the life of every individual. Consequently, cities and houses must be built in accordance with these influences. Religious, magical, and geomantic considerations therefore played an important part. E. B. Havell gives us a translation of some relevant passages from the *Essay on the Architecture of the Hindus* by Ram Raz, published in 1834:

The true position of the cardinal points having been carefully asserted by means of the shadow of a gnomon, rules for the construction of which are given in the Silpasastras, the alignment of the main street of the village was marked out. The general plan of the larger villages followed that of the cosmic cross and the so-called magic square representing the four quarters of the universe; but the reader must not misunderstand this association of mysticism with the practical business of the Indian craftsman. All art in ancient India was held to be magic, and the magic virtues of these figures simply lay in the fact that the experience of many generations had proved that they were best for purposes of defence and gave the most healthy, pleasant and practical layout for an Indian village or town. The easterly axis of the plan ensured that principal streets were purified by the rays of the sun sweeping through them from morning till evening; while the intersection of main streets by shorter ones running north and south provided a perfect circulation of air and the utmost benefit of the cool breezes. . . . In the case of a temple city there were four streets round the temple where the priests and other servants of the temple were accommodated. . . . In the case of a palace the ministers, the advisers, the soldiers guarding the palace, the rich merchants, and the Brahmins were housed in streets planned round the palace.

The layout of the streets was dictated by a magical symbolism that combined long experience with intuition, leading in the end to very practical results:

There should, according to Kautilya, be three ring streets running east and west, and three north and south, consequently twelve gates, three to each side. In Ceylon the streets run generally north and south, east and west, but not with anything like mathematical accuracy. Kurunagala in the fourteenth century had four main streets, according to the "Kurunagala Wistaraya." Since the four streets of the city were made like a lotus flower taken in the hand it is evident those streets radiated from a centre; and since the Brahman's was to the west, Sand street to the east, the street of the Gods to the south, and the Great street to the north it is evident they were arms of a cross pointing to the four quarters. Corresponding to the four gates were four suburbs: the Indian term is "Gate Villages."[1]

On the other hand, purely practical considerations are not neglected:

The plan called Padmaka, after the lotus leaf, is interesting as showing how sedulously Indian town planners avoided the inauspicious layout in which the main streets run upon diagonal lines in the direction of the intermediate points of the compass, the objections to which are not merely sentimental. A plan with streets radiating in all directions from the centre of the village, like spokes of a wheel, would be the first to suggest itself to an Indian designer on account of its symbolism. He avoided it for practical reasons. First, that it was bad for purposes of defence as it gave an enemy many opportunities of establishing himself in the centre of the village by a sudden raid. Secondly, that it tended to the congestion of the traffic and an uncomfortable plan of house and garden especially in the middle of the village. Thirdly, that the streets would mostly run in the wrong direction for the sun.[2]

1. *Ceylon Journal of Science*, 1924–28. Section G, Archeology.
2. Ram Raz, *op. cit.*

The orientation of the houses nevertheless exerts a decisive influence on the layout of the streets. Regarding the importance of the individual house and its place in the plan of the town Ram Raz states: "Just as the village cottage or village hut formed the unit of house-planning, so the village was the unit used to form the mahalla, or ward, in town planning."

C. P. V. Ayyar[3] remarks on the symbolism of the houses:

The dwelling house is constructed on the model of the human body. It must have a doorway and a trellis-work in the wall in the east, and corresponding to the eyes of man two niches in the wall . . . the windows correspond to the nasal cavities. . . . the central courtyard is in the nature of a big lung for the house. It would appear that consciously or unconsciously the conception derived from an acquaintance with the fleshy frame which is the house of the embodied soul has been given a form and a visible representation in the construction of a house, a palace, a temple, and a city. Thus the art of constructing a house does no more than carry farther a process that Nature has already begun.

Islam.   Islamic cities developed mainly either through the influence of agriculture or as nodal points of lines of communication. In the former case they have all the main characteristics of an oasis town; in the latter they are primarily market towns. There are, however, many examples where both factors coincide. Oases are the natural place for the population to congregate and find protection against attacks from hostile neighbors and the inclemency of the desert. Nature and the need of protection combine to produce a concentration of population, with all the consequent drawbacks.

3. *Town Planning in Ancient Dekhan,* 1916.

The towns are not communities in our sense, nor is there anything like an influential guild system as an administrative nucleus that would create a corporate unity. Islam never lost its characteristic social structure; it remained for a long period the religion of a conquering army organized in tribes and clans. The ties of these groups extend beyond the towns and therefore do not contribute to their unification as communities. Instead, there is a tendency toward the formation of groups such as are represented by the different quarters of the town or by unions of craftsmen.

The plan of the towns is not based on a systematically developed street pattern. In general they are divided into business and residential quarters and others that have their origin in religious and family bonds. On the surface Islam is a common-sense religion, eminently in accordance with the demands of daily life, but in its deeper layers magical and fanciful forces are active that only too often make its rational tendencies illusory.

Islam rejects the representation of the human figure. Its artistic creativeness finds its most fruitful field in decorative ornament of an inextricably interwined and ever-renewed multiplicity, and in a literature of profuse fantasy and picturesque description of events. These same features dominate the plan of the Islamic cities, with their maze of narrow, winding lanes irregularly intersected by squares or square-like broadenings. Seen from the air, it would seem almost as though the web of streets had been embossed like an ornament in the coherent mass of the houses.

Neither town nor houses are "extravert"; everything has an "introvert" character: hence, the beautiful inner courtyards and the plain outer walls of the houses, with only the most indispensable openings. The streets are of secondary importance. Their first function is to give access to the houses, and only then do they become lines of communication; even the arterial streets are narrow and curved.

An Islamic city is a grandiose protest against the conditions imposed by Nature, whether it be Toledo, which seems forcibly pressed down on the rocky hill around which the Tagus flows, or any oasis town. The general appearance of an Islamic town is always more or less aggressive, even ruthless; but these very features give it also its vitality and its reality. The main elements are the cell of the house, the center of the bazaar, and the spiritual focus of the mosque. This trinity determines the city's structure and plan. The streets are often directly oriented toward the bazaar; even the blind alleys open only to this side, hardly ever in the opposite direction.

China.   Geomancy and religion also play a very essential part in the foundation and building of the old cities of China. The walls are the most sacred part of the city. They are its cathedral, as it were, the pride of its inhabitants and the symbol of its importance and size. They are erected first, and in many cases they last longer than all the other works, surviving generation after generation. Compared with them, other buildings are almost meaningless.

The city is conceived as a whole from the very beginning, and the space created by the enclosure of the walls is filled only gradually with the houses and official buildings. The walls indicate the standing of the overlord and his city. The Altar of the Earth stands on a small elevation and is square in form. The earth itself is conceived as a square, so the town should have the same shape. As time goes by, the city, as distinct from the castle, the palace of the overlord of early times, gains a more pronounced character of its own. It ceases to be a mere appendix to the palace.

Not unlike the army in its organization, the city is divided into districts and quarters. The parallel to the Roman camp is evident—clear organization, clear planning dominated by a single will—or to the fortress-town of the Renaissance with the *piazza d'armi* in the center. This similarity is especially prominent if a drum tower is erected where the four main streets meet, and if there is "a large fortified four-way gateway which is built over the cross roads so that in times of strife or disorder each street can be isolated from the others."[4]

In the ideal layout, according to ritual laws, the palace is situated right in the center of the city. It is surrounded by walls and forms a city within the city. Every building in the palace compound has its definite place. The residences of the nobles repeat in miniature the arrangement of the prince's palace and are little towns, each surrounded by its own walls. Within these little towns are the compounds of the individual families, each again surrounded by its wall, and repeating all the essential elements of the palace and the residences of the nobles. The whole forms a system consisting of numerous elements, encompassed one by the other, and all oriented towards the palace. It is perhaps the only architectural work whose actual execution corresponds almost entirely with the ideal conception in all its purity. This is a great contrast to the ideal cities of the Renaissance, which were merely designed on paper.

The origin of the Chinese city goes back to a time when life, religion, building, and housing still formed a single whole and religious rites were a reality. The ideal city of the Renaissance, on the other hand, developed out of a program consisting first of all of practical considerations and aesthetic theories of architecture incapable of standing up to the dy-

4. C. P. Fitzgerald, *China.*

namics of life. Peking still stands as a symbol of the Chinese city par excellence; Palma Nova and Gran Michele still stand also, but no one except a few art historians knows of them. Compared with the old towns of China, the towns of the European Middle Ages seem insignificant and small. Their walls are puny in contrast with those of China. Their layout, even if systematic in conception, cannot compete with the grander examples of China.

The European town is the result of rational and economic forces and of a social structure that carried within it from its beginning the germ of disintegration that has ended today in a complete lack of order and unity. Out of the fraternities and guilds of Europe grows the spirit of the middle class entrepreneur and the urban community. Out of the rites of common brotherhood in early China develops neither a feeling of community nor an autonomous local government. The cities of China are not homes of freedom like the urban communities of Europe. They are the seats of the representatives of the central government of the Emperor, and as such they remain nonautonomous. The welfare of a Chinese town depends less on the initiative of its inhabitants than on the efficiency of the imperial administration.

The layout of a Chinese city is developed from the periphery inward: it does not grow outward from the inside. The gates, therefore, are important, and all information about them is valuable, since it reveals the system of the main streets that lead from one gate to another. The south gate is regarded as especially sacred. The north gates usually remain closed, for the north is believed to be full of danger. The main streets form a clear pattern, while the secondary streets within this primary rectangular network are seemingly without system, although they also cross each other at right angles. The reasons for their layout is not intelligible at the first glance.

The houses are the primary element, and the streets are subordinated to their arrangement. Magical considerations play an important part in this respect also. The streets are not curved, but are if necessary bent at right angles. The lanes are often cul-de-sacs. The fact that the entrances to the houses face the south whenever possible is one of the reasons that the layout of the streets appears to be unsystematic and mazelike. In some cases the main streets are oriented in relation to the government building, the *yamen;* they lead directly toward it or pass it on either side.

China is perhaps the only country that was capable of finding an almost final solution of the problem of the relation of house and street. The cities of China—the original, not the Europeanized ones—combine systematic planning in their main principles with great variety of detail. The framework of the main streets and of the walls guarantees all the advantages that arise from conceiving the city as an integrated whole.

Japan.   Although China influenced the planning of Japanese cities—Nara and Old Kyoto are copies of towns of the T'ang dynasty—there is one fundamental difference: Japanese cities have no walls. The foundation of numerous settlements of an urban character during the feudal period proceeded on different lines. Around the castles of the Daimyos developed open settlements of their retainers, the Samurai, professional soldiers. Their houses, together with the castle, were the nucleus around which the peasants erected their homesteads, forming a kind of living wall as a protection for their lord. These settlements were the origin of most Japanese cities.

The tendency towards standardization so characteristic of Japanese civilization is expressed in the house and its standardized size and elements. This uniformity makes it possible to decide the size of a whole town from the number of its houses. As the one-family house is the most common type, the cities would be enormously large were not the houses small.

An indirect consequence of this standardization is that it is not the streets but the blocks themselves, or whole quarters, that serve as means of orientation. The streets are more or less passive interspaces, with no special significance. They cross each other almost always at right angles; they run mostly from north to south and from east to west, thus producing a checker board pattern. In general there is more rigidity in the street system of the Japanese than in the Chinese cities. The grandeur of China is missing, and the greater standardization of the house makes it more liable to a certain subordination to the street. But the house itself is one of the most beautiful products of domestic architecture. It is generally oriented toward the south, and house and garden are intimately related to each other. Many windows and doors open out onto even the smallest garden space. In spite of the not very imaginative general layout, the house remains the primary element in the planning of the city.

Greece.   The Greek *polis* was limited both in size and character. It was the reflection of the tendency to develop a balanced social structure within definite boundaries and to fix its scale in general and in detail by man's own standards. Aristotle demands that the *polis* should house "the largest number which suffices for the purpose of life and can be taken in at a single view." The result is that the *polis* did not grow without restriction. If the population exceeded a certain number, a new *polis* was founded. This idea of limitation dominates Greek town planning to such a degree that, to give only one example, Syracuse at the time of its greatest extension consisted of five different "towns," each surrounded by its own wall. Strabo calls it Pentapolis.

A very sound idea lay at the root of this principle: that of decentralization through the founding of new cities, either near the old site or as more distant colonies. This was especially evident in the colonial countries. First, for instance, Kyme was founded; then, when it reached what was considered an appropriate size, Puteoli was laid out a mile away; then the first Neapolis in the same direction; and when this also reached its limit, a new Neapolis sprang up in the immediate neighborhood, so that the earlier Newtown became Palaeopolis.

The *polis* developed in opposition to the countryside, but unlike the medieval city of Continental Europe it did not express this antagonism in surrounding walls. Only later was such protection added. In the *polis* life went on mostly outside the house. In the medieval town, the house is the home of the burgher; men gather there for special purposes. The houses of the *polis* jostled each other; there were no gardens, or only interior ones, within the precincts of the houses. The town of the early Middle Ages was a garden city; the private garden was an effective instrument of segregation and a promoter of privacy.

The continuous colonnades of the Greek *polis* were the embodiment of the community life. Originally "agora" meant "assembly" and later "assembly-place," but not "market square." The market square of a medieval town is first of all a space for a definite economic purpose, which is in many cases the *raison d'être* of the town. Out of the club-life of the Greeks developed the spirit of the city-state; out of the narrow sphere of the guilds grows the spirit of the parochial burgher.

Up to the time of Alexander the Great the *polis* was a coastal town, only one day's journey from the sea. Consequently the Mediterranean was the field of extension of the *polis*. The typical medieval town is, except in a few cases, an inland city, and may expand either through its own enlargement or by gaining a territorial hegemony over its hinterland. It is for these reasons that the surrounding territory belonged to the *polis* as an integral part of it, whereas the medieval town forms a kind of association with its hinterland within the territory of the State.

It is irrelevant to argue whether the regular preceded the irregular town plan or the reverse. Everywhere we find both side by side, but gradually the checkerboard layout gained the upper hand. It is connected with the name of Hippodamos; but it is very doubtful that he was the first to apply this principle systematically. In contrast to the Roman town, which is surrounded by walls from the very beginning —the sacred rite of marking out the area by outlining the circumvallation with a plow is well known—the walls were not the primary elements of the *polis*. The limitation of its size rested on the idea that life itself should flow within a well-balanced orbit. As Aristotle expressed it in the Nichomachean Ethics: "Evil is a form of the unlimited, and good of the limited." Smallness and limitation were a moral tenet.

For the Romans this idea was not sufficient as an integrating force. They organized the spiritual factor, as it were, in order to make it actually visible and to exert a concrete influence on the inhabitants. Therefore we find within the outer walls the distinct cross of the main streets. To the Romans organization meant everything, while to the Greeks instinctive empathy was the driving power out of which their specific "realism" developed.

If we take this characteristic difference into account, it is easier to understand the principles underlying the Greek checkerboard plan. It is an assemblage of individual elements, of block units. The Greek checkerboard plan is not essentially a net of streets like that of the Romans, where the ground pattern of streets crossing each other at right angles is the primary factor, and the built-up blocks are a mere residue whose shape and size are determined by the rigid layout of the street ribbons.

Miletus, which is said to owe its layout to Hippodamos, had no main axis. The public buildings were not organically related to the plan as a whole. The number of block units could be increased *ad libitum* by external addition, though this would not produce an organic growth of the town from within. However, this was not done; the idea of the *polis* forbade it. When in the later periods a wall was built, it was a protection rather than a means of limitation. Just as expansion in general proceeded by the repetition of the *"polis"* leading to the foundation of new towns, so in detail the "block unit" was the element of planning. Repetition and imitation occured because thinking in abstract space relations was not yet a matter of course. "What is not, is unthinkable" was the dictum of Parmenides.

The mere addition of adjacent units was, therefore, the appropriate solution of architectural problems. The child puts his little bricks together to build a toy town without attaching any meaning to the space between them. The Greek temple stands in the landscape like a sculpture; it is not the expression of a feeling of space. Likewise, the situation of the block units is conceived in the spirit of sculpture. The streets as space do not exist; they are not a spatial element of any significance.

Quite different is the Roman attitude, symbolized by the Pantheon. The interior surrounded by a shell is the essential; so it was with the streets of a Roman city. The first step in the development of a city was the layout of the streets, that is, of the space between the built-up blocks. As Lao-tse said: "It is on the space where there is nothing that the utility of the house depends." Thus, Greek sculpture stands in contrast to Roman space. Sculpture needs no "limitation"; it is limited in itself. Space needs limitation in order to be functionally effective. Sculptures can be put side by side. Space can be subdivided and limited.

MEDIEVAL CITIES

After the steamroller of the Great Migrations had laid the visible remnants of the civilization of the Roman Empire in ruins, and the development of agriculture had again reached a more advanced stage, the first signs of urban life reappeared, and with them the burgher of the Middle Ages. His life was carried on within the limited living-space of his town, which he created in opposition to and with almost revolutionary determination against the peasants and feudal lords. He was able to achieve this end successfully because to his new creation, the town, he confined his spiritual and practical activities. He adapted its social and economic structure to this limited sphere; and out of this self-restraint grew the unerring conviction that his town was the center on which everything was focused.

His conception of the world hardly differed from that of Aristotle. For him too the earth was the center of the universe, which he conceived as a gigantic sphere enclosing it. Yet the self-reliance of the Greeks and their positive attitude toward life had given way to a profound diffidence. Medieval man was faced with perplexities which threatened to undermine the unity of his religious faith with his practical life. These disruptive forces drove him into fraternal association with his fellow-citizens, in the hope of finding mental and spiritual balance and a lessening of individual responsibility by allegiance to organized groups within the town. He needed the visible limitation of his community by a wall, which was above all the expression of this mental attitude. He needed the human scale as yardstick for the extension of his town, which was made for pedestrians; and within this external protecting shell he needed the internal shells of the guild and family. He needed the Church, but he placed beside it administrative buildings, the town hall and the guildhalls.

For a considerable time, within the towns north of the Alps, numerous open spaces were left for agriculture and horticulture, and here and in Italy the inhabitants owned land outside the walls. In the beginning the towns were to a certain degree self-supporting. However, this grew less true as time went on. The growing importance of the towns was the direct outcome of a well-balanced social structure that enabled them to fulfill their tasks efficiently. Not only was the population moderate in numbers, but its composition corresponded most advantageously to their main purpose, that of being the active agent of a new economic order. While the inhabitant of the *polis* has been described as a *zoon politikon,* his medieval successor may be called a *zoon oikonomikon.*

The structure of the town eliminated all that did not belong to it; it used everything that was needed; and it was stratified within itself in such a way that it could live and let live, and its citizens could rely on a decent income. Social and economic differences were relatively small, as a result of the limited size of the towns and of the ties between the individual and his professional group. Like the *polis,* the medieval town did not grow beyond a certain size, and extensions took place only in later periods, under strong pressure of population. As in Greece, this limitation often led to the foundation of new towns.

Man as an individual was more important in the town than in the country; he was a voluntary and free member of urban society. It is this freedom, which did not exist for the peasants, that made the towns at once powerful and attractive. They were places where organized and skilled workmanship was carried on on a religious and ethical basis. The development of medieval towns is part of the historical change which leads from time to time to a wide decentralization of the population over a large area, or to its concentration in a restricted number of places, depriving the countryside of many of its people and thus retarding its population growth.

Because of inadequate communications the towns were rather isolated from each other. In most cases the distance between two neighboring towns could be covered by foot in both directions in one day. This again gave each inhabitant a feeling of security within his own walls. The medieval town was small. "It can be taken in in one view." The middle-sized town of Central Europe did not cover an average area of more than 125 acres, while small towns covered only 10 to 25 acres, though these were later very densely built up. Within such small dimensions the wall was an ever-present reality.

The appearance of the town gradually changed. During the early period, large spaces that were not built over were a characteristic feature, and the burghers were engaged, to some extent, in agricultural pursuits. There was at least a garden to the house, or some fields, outside the narrower sphere of the town, were cultivated. It is partly for these reasons that in many towns of the early period there was no market square. The industrial activities of the townspeople were still too rudimentary, and agriculturally the town was still more self-supporting than it became later. The need of exchanging goods between town and country was not yet great enough to justify the layout of a special market square; if there was one at all, it was only small.

By way of exception there were the large market places east of the Elbe, sometimes up to five acres in extent; they served as cattle markets or as sites for the fairs. With the growth of urban industry and the decline of the cattle market, buildings and booths for the weekly market, which later became permanent houses, and other edifices, such as market scales and offices, were erected. If the remaining space became too small, a new market was developed. In general the medieval town, in accordance with its rational layout, had no open spaces or pleasure-gardens but only spaces for practical purposes. Growth of the urban population, through new-comers, and of the industrial arts led to increased subdivision of the urban area. More and more craftsmen became owners of houses and land, and in this way they became attached to the urban soil—a reversal of the all too common idea that the town "uproots" its inhabitants.

The urban society of the Middle Ages did not consist, as do our present urban masses, of human atoms held together primarily by economic, class, and professional interests. It was built up of groups in which the individual was embedded both in general and in detail. Family, guilds, religious orders, and confraternities enclosed him; ties of blood sheltered him, as well as those of work, class, and religion. It was no single one of these attachments but the complex of them all that created both the order of life in the medieval town and its physical plan. A fully developed town was a union, in the sense of a brotherhood, not unlike the *polis*. The God of the town, or its Saint, in each case united and protected the citizens.

In contrast with all previous religions, Christianity broke up the magical and tabooist links on which blood relationship largely rests in India, China, Japan, in the Islamic countries, and partly in Russia. Under the guidance of the Church, elective affinity took the place of consanguineous relationship. This voluntary association gave a new security and was primarily instrumental in the creation of an urban *community*, which in countries such as those mentioned above exists not at all or only in a very modified form.

The typical medieval dwelling was the small, narrow house owned by those who lived in it. It determined the general layout of the town and its subdivision. The rooms were arranged one behind the other; they were not as yet lined up along a corridor. The windows were relatively small. Place of work and living rooms were under the same roof. The whole was a perfect "dwelling machine," functional, spacious, and intimate. The house was the primary element in the plan of the town. This explains its seemingly unsystematic appearance. In reality the layout of a medieval town is one of the most systematic in the whole history of town planning. This very recognition of the primacy of the houses produced the distinctive functionalism which is one of the main characteristics of the towns of the Middle Ages, although it is not apparent to a superficial observer. There is a marked difference between the main streets and those which open up the remaining spaces between them. There are short blind alleys, closes, all kinds of streets and small squares, serving most efficiently the community's purposes. Traffic and residential streets are clearly distinguished as a result of this profoundly practical approach.

The medieval town is the last example of a functional balance between houses and streets. The beginning of the end was in the Cult of the Street, although this development is not apparent at first glance. Yet it is a fact, in spite of all the grandiose performances of architects and town planners, especially during the *Renaissance* and *Baroque* periods. It is a sunset majestic in its beauty—but a sunset it is. In the end it leads to the empty plans of the vista-mongers of the present day, and to the inefficiency of streets and houses alike because of failure to recognize the fundamental principles governing their respective functions.

RENAISSANCE
AND BAROQUE CITIES

The year 1543 is a decisive turning point. In this year Copernicus' treatise *De Revolutionibus* was published. It stated openly what many had already been feeling unconsciously for a long time. The Renaissance began. The earth was removed from its central place in the system of the universe. The ancient conception of the world became meaningless. Man could no longer see it as if from its center; he was moved with the earth itself to the periphery. In 1610 Rome stated that:

to assert that the sun stands immovably in the center of the universe is absurd, philosophically wrong, and a formal heresy, since it is in flagrant contradiction to the Holy Scriptures. To assert that the earth is not fixed in the center of the universe, that it is not immovable but even revolves each day on its own axis, is absurd, philosophically wrong, at least an incorrect belief.

If the great ones of this world chose to adhere to this conviction it was hardly possible to expect the simple citizens to be less traditional. Small wonder, then, that the towns and their inhabitants changed but slowly, quite apart from the very slow development of the art of city planning itself.

Only on February 17, 1600, was the way toward the modern age entirely cleared. On this day Giordano Bruno was burnt at the stake in the Campo di Fiori. He was the first to assert that the sphere of the fixed stars is not the limit of the world; that the world has no limits, but is infinite. He, too, only expressed the general feeling that life in a narrow sphere is unbearable and that a free and wider view is essential. The shell-like limitations were bursting; the expanding influence of the towns and the breaking up of the guilds and of their coercive unification were being, as it were, officially justified. Only now did the development of the medieval town really come to an end; only now were its

burghers losing their revolutionary urge and exchanging it
for a narrow parochialism.

At this hour modern man was born, and with him developed a new attitude towards life, that of the Renaissance
and the Baroque. Yet with it spread the influence of the
State, and the free burgher became an obedient subject. The
simple limitation of the towns came to an end; it gave way
to a complicated system of defense which would withstand
more efficiently the new technique of the far-reaching fire-
arms. The perspective view, the outlook over a wide area,
became the accepted principle of city planning.

In the Middle Ages the ring of walls was laid out while
the town was gradually taking shape. With the Renaissance
a new development set in, characterized by a different procedure: the military engineer fixed the *enceinte* first, and
only then did he design within it the plan of the city, adapting it to this surrounding belt. The beginning of this period
coincided with a new theory of city planning that demonstrated its main principles in the design of Ideal Cities. A
new limitation now restricted the growth of many urban
communities that had just begun to breathe more freely in
spite of their walled-in existence. The extension of a city
was not so easy and simple as before. The fortifications were
too complicated and expensive. On the other hand a few
places took over the protection of others, so that the walls of
these latter became unnecessary.

Together with the wall the meaning and layout of the
streets were changing. The streets assumed primary importance, and the blocks of houses were fitted in between them
without much consideration for the basic requirements of
the houses themselves. A perspective view was desired, and
for this throughfares were needed. The web of streets was

the main characteristic of the plan. The old center, the market square, the church, the town hall, and the guild halls lost their importance and ceased to be essential elements in the layout. The periphery became more significant.

But aesthetically everything was still at rest; it had not yet been drawn into the vortex so characteristic of the Baroque. Yet men felt that the old values were disintegrating and the old theories out of date. Only a few realized that man and the reality of life alone are the active instruments which change the conception and appearance of the city. G. Botero stated this clearly in his *Treatise Concerning the Causes of the Magnificence and Greatness of Cities* published in 1606:

A city is said to be an assembly of people, a congregation drawn together, to the end they may thereby the better live at their ease in wealth and plenty. And the greatness of a city is said to be not the largeness of the site or the circuit of the walls, but the multitude and number of inhabitants and their power. Now men are drawn together upon sundry causes and occasions thereunto them moving, some by authority, some by force, some by pleasure and some by profit. Let no man think that a city may go on in increase without ceasing. Some answer, the cause hereof is the plague, the wars, the dearths—some others say, it is because God the governor of all things does so dispose. I say that the augmentation of cities proceeds partly out of the virtues generative of men, and partly out of the virtues nutritive of the cities.

The town burgher, the group-individual, changed into the loyal citizen of the State or the subject of a prince, the latter being especially characteristic of Central Europe and Italy. These new trends emerged only slowly, and were first expressed in a decay of the old ideas and institutions rather than in a determined acceptance of the new ones. The world

of unquestioning and faithful reliance on the religious doctrines of the Church of Rome did not quickly fall to pieces;
the anthropocentric conception of the universe had pene-
trated too deeply into the life and mind of humanity. To go
on living within narrow limitations was so much more convenient than to face the problems of the newly-gained
"infinity."

At first only a few dared to think freely and to acknowl-
edge the new reality. Others fell in with the altered course
more instinctively, making use of the numerous possibilities
that offered themselves. This vanguard consisted of the
spiritual and social *élite* of the great discoverers and inven-
tors and the princes. Prince and State were identical; *l'état
c'est moi*. But the prince of the Baroque was not like the
despot of ancient times; he was not prince and God in one.
He was merely the apex of the social pyramid. The palace of
the princes was not the center of the city; it was the beginning and the end of the perspective view. Versailles and
Karlsruhe are the best-known examples. In Karlsruhe the
palace was planned and built first, and the town, with its 32
radial streets converging on the palace, was only later added
as an appendix to the residence of the prince. The task of
the city planners was to create not one center but several
"centers" in the form of *rond points*.

The essence of the cities of this time can be fully understood, however, only by taking into account the tensions
which arose out of the new attitude to life during the Baroque period. These tensions resulted from a changed conception of space, that is to say, from thinking and planning
on a larger scale. They resulted from the growing knowledge
that the world is so complex that its innumerable potentialities can be mastered and usefully employed only by com-

bining on the same level the sense of reality and the sense of possibility, theory and practice, planning and execution, imagination and sobriety. The symbols of this combination are Don Quixote and Sancho Panza.

The new idea of space was almost the reverse of that of the Gothic period. The interior of the cathedrals, which seemed to lose all substantiality and to dematerialize the surrounding matter, fundamentally changed. Now the limitless expanse of the sky was painted on the material shell of the domes of the churches. The mystical transcendence permeating the Gothic cathedrals was replaced by an ostentatious and festive atmosphere to the glory of God, which gives the Baroque churches an unreal and yet earthly excitement. Men respond to the new spaciousness without desiring to be lost in it. Men wanted reality without giving up the new possibilities. Baroque works have something hollow and exaggerated about them. They are full of ambitious emotions that no one could endure in reality.

In place of the mendicant orders, the aristocratic Jesuits held the attention of urban society. They made faith "palatable," or, in other words, leveled it down. It is no mere chance that a number of the most famous artists, such as Rubens, Van Dyck, and Bernini, were in close contact with the Jesuits. Art became a means of propaganda for the Society of Jesus. Bernini is the prototype of the artist for whom the end justified every means. There is the same pretentious *élan*, spaciousness, theatrical aplomb, propagandist allurement, and desire to fly away into the unlimited sky— but there the urge ends. Andrea del Pozzo, also associated with the Jesuits, was the founder of a systematic doctrine of perspective and of a fake architecture, in brief, of illusion, of the "as if." The interior of the Gesù, with its contrast between the dome concentrating the light and the obscure side-aisles, is the perfect embodiment of these tendencies; it is a magnificent theater. Only an organization which had developed so high a standard of theater and opera performances as the Jesuits could have inspired the building of this church.

The decline of the Church meant the rise of the State, and with it of capitalism. The extraordinary and swift development of the medieval towns had come to an end long ago. The establishment of new cities was relatively rare. In most cases, already existing places were merely extended. Some towns became centers of the new State administration. The bond between the cities and their immediate hinterland grew laxer, not so much because direct exchange of goods between them ceased as because the influence of the cities was spreading over greater distances, and improved communications made it possible to buy and sell in many different and more distant places.

The centralizing tendencies of the State were gradually replacing the equal status of numerous cities by a kind of hierarchy; a restricted number of cities became more important and took the lead. Their population increased faster than that of the others. But in spite of the growing power of the State, some cities embarked on an almost imperialistic policy of their own, suppressing their weaker neighbors in order to barter away their political privileges to the princes or the king. With this development came a certain specialization of towns into fortress towns, commercial towns, industrial towns, and so on.

City planning became an instrument of State policy, a tendency which was favored by the actual situation: the theory of city planning, widely discussed in speech and writing, demanded a systematic expression. This was perfectly natural in order to meet the requirements of the changing technique of defense, the desire for display, and the idea of perspective. Pageantry is always connected with systematic preparation; we may cite as an example the rehearsal for the last coronation in England, or the "spontaneous" mass demonstrations in totalitarian states.

An impressive perspective view can be achieved only through wide streets and correspondingly laid-out squares and through viewpoints systematically distributed within them or at their ends, that is, by methodical previous planning and not by unregulated growth. Special consideration was given to the layout of homogeneous squares surrounded on all sides by uniformly designed buildings (such as the Palace Vendôme or the Place des Vosges in Paris), to wide and uninterrupted streets, to the extension of cities under the supervision of the State in accordance with definite plans, and to the erection of rows of private houses conforming to a single pattern. Everything was liable to regimentation. The bylaws of the time do not leave much liberty in general or in detail. The case of Mannheim at the beginning of the eighteenth century is typical: among other things we may note the fixed orientation and height of the buildings, the height and number of stories, the depth of the buildings, the shape of the roofs, the situation and size of the front doors and windows, the prohibition of all external decoration, and so on, in order "to make the whole street appear one house."

England occupied a somewhat different position. In the eighteenth century, England's influence on city planning was on the upgrade, especially through two principles still manifest today: the interspersal of open spaces in the layout of the town and the unification of whole streets by homogeneous architecture of the private houses.

Abstract geometrical patterns were essential elements of the city-planning schemes. Whether the system of streets was a radial or a checkerboard one, both had in common the central square, the *piazza d'armi*, on which the streets converged. Medieval fortifications did not, at least in principle, exert a decisive influence on the layout. Now the central square became fundamentally a mere meeting point of a number of streets that ran to important parts of the circumvallation. The *piazza d'armi*, the rallying point for defense, was the city's center because from it all parts of the fortifications could be reached equally quickly through the streets leading in a straight line towards the periphery. The task of combining architectural beauty and the requirements of defense was described by Palladio:

The main traffic and commercial streets of the town should be wide and adorned with stately buildings; for in this way the visitors will get a more impressive idea of the town and often think that the other parts of it are equally beautiful. The main streets, which we shall call military streets, should be laid out in such a way that they follow their course without any divergence, leading in a straight line from the gates to the central square, and if possible continue the straight line further to the opposite gate. In accordance with the size of the town several smaller squares should intersect these streets. Moreover, the important streets should be oriented not only in relation to the main square but also the main buildings such as churches, palaces, arcades and other buildings.

At the beginning of the eighteenth century France took the lead in the theoretical approach to city planning. Daviler writes:

From the architectural point of view a town is a complex of buildings arranged symmetrically and beautifully, and of streets and public squares laid out along a building line in an appealing and healthy arrangement and with the necessary incline for drainage. The most beautiful streets are those which are straightest and widest.

This last demand is quite in conformity with the ideas of the time, but it has exerted a devastating effect up to the present day. Germany followed the same line. I. F. Penther remarks laconically in his *Lexicon architectonicum* (1744) under the heading "Street". "The wider and more straight a street, the more beautiful it is."

In the Middle Ages the pedestrian fixed the scale; now the carriage, although used only by the rich, was the important factor, since the upper classes exerted a decisive influence upon the life of the city and its architecture. Everything seemed restless. The streets do not invite a leisurely stroll; the perspective view and the monotony of the long rows of more or less identical houses appear to possess a motive power that concentrates the attention almost exclusively on the view at the end of the streets and induces a steady forward movement. It was the beginning of that Cult of the Street which is still in full swing today. The streets were not interrupted by bends, breaks, or any other kind of diversion; they were broken at intervals by architectural accents such as fountains, obelisks, *rond points*, and squares where they met other streets, but their straight lines were preserved.

The width of the streets is in many cases quite disproportionate to their actual purpose. The demand was for spaciousness at any price. Sometimes this demand went so far that existing buildings were pulled down in order to gain more space or to open out the view of a more important building, even at the cost of spoiling its architectural balance with its surroundings. Another characteristic feature was the erection of façades, with the rooms behind arranged independently of the external appearance of the house, and therefore without system, or an interspace between two houses, closed by a front wall crowned by the principal cornice, in order to give the impression of an uninterrupted block front. The most outspoken example of this building from outside to inside is the Place Vendôme. The façades surrounding it were built at the expense of Louis XIV, while the houses behind them were paid for by private persons who each bought "a length of façade" of from two to ten windows.

Streets and squares formed a geometrical pattern; small wonder in a time when mathematics began to mean so much. The step thence to a symbolism of numbers as an element of city planning is but a very small one. Conceiving and looking at the plan arouses something of the aesthetic delight of the reality. The military engineers in particular were devoted to this symbolism of numbers. Seven plays a great role in Holland; it is the number of the United Provinces. Thus, we find seven bastions in some of the fortress towns, for example, Willemstad, Coevorden, Deventer, and Enkhuizen. Groningen had seventeen bastions corresponding to its seventeen counties, influenced also by the sacred character attributed to this number. In Italy, Alberti designed the town of Palma Nova with nine bastions in honor of the nine families of the Venetian hereditary nobility.

The drawing-board scheme dominated city planning. It was inelastic and stereotyped, less adaptable than the plan of the medieval town with its engirdling walls. Uniformity was thought necessary for freedom of movement, and the adaptation to the site and to individual needs that gave the medieval town such a direct immediateness and intimacy was not in accord with the spirit and temper of the new time. There was a gain in breadth of imagination and feeling, but it was felt that both were valuable only if they were disciplined.

The increasing concentration of capital and the greater mobility of money as a means of exchange led to speculation in urban sites. In consequence of this development the poorer quarters were separated from those of the rich; the former were more densely built up than the latter. The poorer classes were restricted to the older and less healthy quarters, or housed in new dwellings erected as objects of speculation. However, there ran parallel with these trends, especially in Germany, a land policy systematically directed by the State and conducted with the aim of eliminating, as far as possible, the ill effects of *laissez faire*.

During the seventeenth and eighteenth centuries new cities and extensions of existing ones were built on public land owned by the State or the prince or by the cities themselves. The cities were empowered to acquire private land under favorable conditions, in many cases for no more than its agricultural value. The differentiation between residential and traffic streets disappeared; it was superseded by a uniform pattern in which every street could serve as either or both. A valuable element was thus lost for a long time to European city planning.

The new social and economic order had a far-reaching effect upon the relationship among the places in which men lived, worked, and sold. The market square lost its importance: it was used principally for buying and selling food. Shops made their appearances. "Shops" had existed before this, but they were rather primitive and usually consisted of only one room adjoining the workshop in the craftsman's house, if there was even a separate room at all. The medieval "shopkeeper" would keep some goods "in stock" or put a few of his products in the window. There were also market halls for single commodities such as cloth, furs, shoes, bread, and grain. Now sale and production, home and workshop separated.

These changes considerably influenced the structure of the town and the houses. Life was divided between the dwelling place and the office or workshop, and though the distances were still short, some time had to be spent on the daily journey to and from the place of work. Family life and business life fell apart. The need for communications grew. In general, one walked for short distances. Only a small number of carriages were in use, and they were far beyond the means of the average tradespeople.

Nevertheless, the restful and stationary life of the Middle Ages, and its tranquil confinement within the circles of family, guild, Church, and the walls of the town, was broken up and its pace was accelerated. Personal life and working life lost their mutual balance; work became the center around which everything else rotated till it swallowed up the whole of man's thinking and feeling, his loyalty and interests, and dictated the cycle of his daily life; till fragmentary man, the finished product of our own time, emerged, and functional life gained an absolute ascendancy.

The new town house, especially on the Continent, was wider than the medieval house, and turned its eaves instead of its gable to the street. Italian influences played their part; the castles of the feudal lords of the Middle Ages gave place to the palaces of the town. The windows were larger and the whole building more adapted to juxtaposition with other buildings. Houses of these types, placed preferably in the main streets, appear more imposing than they really are. The individual house was now a subordinate part of a complete block front. Just as it had changed its outside, so its interior took on a totally different structure. The Baroque prefers to arrange the rooms along a corridor and to specialize them for different purposes. Such houses were eminently suited for division into several units. They usher in the era of the flat. Living accommodation of this kind was needed especially for the growing number of officials and military personnel. Smaller and narrower houses were built for craftsmen and the lower middle class.

Another important feature of city planning can also be traced back to this period. Verdure penetrates the city. This development, at least in its more essential aspects, derived its main impetus from the palace gardens. In the seventeenth century most of the pleasure gardens were situated outside the cities proper. Trees were not yet used in laying out the streets and squares. It was only in the eighteenth century that a change took place. The new ideas were applied even to so-called colonial towns, such as the military settlements founded by Maria Theresa in the eastern frontier districts of her Empire, or Carouge near Geneva designed by Laurent Giardine in 1784. Instead of walls, double lines of trees surround the city, and in some parts penetrate even to the center. At the same time interest in private gardens was reawakening.

The seventeenth century rationalized the natural surroundings. It imposed a geometrical pattern on Nature. This is evident, for instance, in Amsterdam, in the adaptation of the banks of the canals to the standardized pattern of the circular and radial streets. It can also be seen in the most representative example, the park of Versailles, laid out on a site only very poorly endowed by Nature. Nature is a stimulus to the creation of something new; therefore, we find this forcible reshaping of Nature, if for no other reason than for the sake of a rigid layout; therefore, also, the rational trimmings of the hedges and trees.

In the eighteenth century this picture changed, under English influence. The garden was assimilated to Nature—"corrected" only in so far as seems essential in order to soften her wild and unmodified originality and to gain a perspective view. But this idea itself had changed: in Versailles, broad vistas are dominating factors in the whole layout, while the English landscape gardener utilized natural features to the utmost, preferring silhouettes of large groups of trees, one behind the other, and relating the distant views opened up between these groups to his general scheme in such a way that they were merely one but not the dominating element. There, the unbroken view; here, the subdivision of the distant view. There, the impression of depth; here, the impression of coulisses arranged *en échelon*.

But not only did the garden change; the relationship between the general layout of the city and Nature underwent a far-reaching transformation. There was a revolt against rigidity, against monotonous standardization. In contrast to Karlsruhe and Versailles, Bath was developed. Man utilized the natural features to enhance the effect of the buildings; he lived closer to Nature. In a more liberated atmosphere the medieval walls, the Renaissance *enceinte* of fortifications, the deadening rigidity of the stereotyped pattern of the Baroque, had now really and definitely fallen. The spread of the modern cities over the countryside had begun.

The period of *laissez faire* was approaching, though the State was still regarded as absolute. The scientific foundations of this new conception were the laws of Newton. They define the world as a harmonious entity, all of whose parts are working systematically in a dynamic balance. God has created the world, but it runs smoothly and efficiently by its own power. The relationship between the State and society is viewed in the same way. The State has given birth to new economic activities. This is enough. Now it should resign and interfere no longer, in order to give free rein to a laissez-faire economy. Society is good enough as it is. It rests quite naturally on the principle of "the two nations," the wealthy and the poor.

Montesquieu is only expressing this general conviction when he says: *il faut bien qu'il y ait du luxe. Si les riches n'y depensent pas beaucoup, les pauvres mourront de faim.* The passion for luxury was growing, especially in the large cities. The elements of the modern machinery of entertainment appeared, and with them the problem of leisure—in our sense. Theaters, music and dance halls, fashionable restaurants, elegant shops, hotels, and less expensive establishments of all kinds were springing up for the less favored classes.

MODERN CITIES

The period from the close of the Renaissance to the French Revolution laid the foundation for many problems of city planning which are facing us today. The originally beneficial legacies of the sixteenth, seventeenth and eighteenth centuries have changed into gifts from the Greeks because we are clinging to them too long and too persistently. The results are devastating. Never before have men's living and working places been more unsystematically lumped together; never before have houses and streets so completely lost their functional significance. Never before has an uncultured atmosphere of such brute intensity dominated the layout and architectural appearance of our cities. The fact that we have got so used to the monstrosities and discrepancies of our physical environment that we hardly realize them is no excuse, nor does it make a radical break with these conditions less urgent.

Many people will think that this is an overstatement, and that our cities are not so bad after all, especially if they are given a slight overhaul. But there are also many who will agree that this harsh judgment is justified. Today we have arrived at a point where new and more creative forces are just beginning to emerge. This is a hopeful sign. But to all who are not biased it is evident beyond a doubt that city planning reached its lowest level during the last hundred years. The greatest compliment that could be paid to it would be silence. But this, unfortunately, is impossible, for the ill effects of a century's mismanagement and muddle exert a most deplorable influence on all plans for a new start.

The age of *laissez faire* was an interruption of the steady development of collective effort that had been taking place since the beginning of the Middle Ages. In this respect the nineteenth century may be compared to a pioneering enterprise on a gigantic scale. This may be a welcome explanation and excuse for many who are more tolerant. But the fact remains that this period possesses all the characteristics of such a pioneer undertaking: lack of foresight, of right judgment, and of objectives clearly defined and appreciated. In a society as complex as ours has become, the control of environment is conditioned by collective considerations that diminished the freedom of individual action. This means that a systematic coordination of the many forces shaping our environment is essential, and that all are interdependent.

Under these conditions it is only natural that today neither streets nor houses fulfill their purpose. Some of the reasons for their decline in functional efficiency need explanation, at least in broad outline, if we are to discover the most useful starting point for a new endeavor.

For the second time the townsman is the agent of a far-reaching revolutionary transformation. Just as in the Middle Ages the burgher created his town in opposition to the feudal lords and the peasants, alone and unaided by the State, so now the citizen builds the modern city. But there is this difference—nothing opposes him. The State assists his work, and he for his part uses the State in his own interests. Nineteenth-century man felt hardly any doubts of his mission. But today scepticism and diffidence are finding their way into the minds of many, and are making mankind ripe for great changes. In this process technique has played a prominent part.

The city of the "practical" and "technically minded" drawing-board architect and road builder has come into being. Streets and traffic, tenement houses and block systems are presented as purely technical, not as social problems. Streets are built with all kinds of pipe systems and other utility services ready-made, so that a sufficient number will be "in stock" when the need arises. People speculate in

suburban sites; jerry-built houses are erected on the con-
veyer-belt.

But we forget that human beings are not cattle, and
that their social needs are not a mere by-product which can
be thrust aside without detrimental effects. The inhabitants
of the city and of the individual houses are not the primary
concern of these city planners and speculators, but are mere
pawns in the game of *laissez faire.* The contrast with the
Greek *polis* is now enormous. The development of the city
has passed far beyond the medieval town, with its narrow
hinterland, through the fortress town of the Renaissance and
the residential town of the absolute prince, both of them
clearly limited entities, until it has lost the last vestiges of any
limitation and distinct shape and has spilt over into the
countryside.

The modern city is not a social community. At best it is
an association of different classes of society on an economic
basis, at worst an agglomeration of human atoms. Under
such conditions no clear conception can arise of what a city
should be. In practice only a few details, such as the width
of the streets and the nature of the sanitary installations, are
objects of administrative interest. The overvaluing of technical and economic problems entirely prohibits any right
understanding of what our cities should be. Though they are
the characteristic expression of our time, they have neither
organic structure nor definite architectural form.

The improvement in means of communication has so far
resulted in little more than an unsystematic increase of urban
traffic and a dense concentration of population, each factor
contributing toward the development of large blocks of flats
and, in the end, of skyscrapers. But the fundamental cause
of this process is the speculative exploitation of urban land

and houses as objects of private profit. Both land and houses are primary requirements, indispensable consumers' goods, and as such their price ought not to depend on the "Law of Supply and Demand."

Moreover, one of the arguments in favor of this process is that a more intensive use of land, that is, a more densely built-up area, reduces the share of the price of the land falling on each individual flat or house. This argument is false. On the contrary, the price rises in direct relation to the increased use of the land. At the same time traffic improvement has produced a misconceived decentralization. It has driven the population to the periphery of the cities and is the direct cause of their sprawling tendencies, of ribbon development and suburbia. The essential place of traffic in relation to city planning has been misunderstood: traffic should not be increased *ad libitum*, but reduced by an intelligent layout of the city and a sound land policy.

There would seem to be four main principles in prewar city planning. There is first the attempt to find some kind of balance between the circular and the radial tendencies that govern the extension of the cities. Then there is the changing relationship between center and periphery. In the past the center was favored as the residential quarter, and the outskirts were regarded as less suitable for this purpose. This holds good for both the Middle Ages and the Renaissance. In the Baroque the better quarters were grouped around the palace and were, therefore, situated away from the center. In modern times the central part is only in a very small degree residential; that function has been taken over by the outlying districts. The centripetal structure has given way to a centrifugal one. This is mainly a result of the third principle, the separation of home from place of work. The fourth factor is the preponderance of the small dwelling unit for the mass of the people. This very generalized classification will serve as framework for the discussion that follows.

The General Plan. France provides diagonal streets and *rond points,* but contributes hardly anything to the development of open spaces. Vienna inaugurates the *Ringstrasse,* the circular road. Germany and America produce the checkerboard pattern. In addition to this, the former introduces the romantic element of the curved street, while the latter's contribution to this international hotch-potch is the park system. England's share is the garden suburb and the garden city. All these together have produced the horrible higgledly-piggledy in which we live.

A good deal of the nineteenth century had still to pass before the old conception of the concentric development of a city lost its hold over the mind of the responsible authorities and of the man in the street. Both material and ideal forces were exerting their influence in favor of a circular restriction. The sites of former fortifications were used for open spaces or circular roads, for the building of circular railway lines, or as a belt of open space outside the built-up area. The circular concept determined the administrative boundaries of the community, the zone of the communal taxes and rates, investment through the rising prices of the land in the outer districts as the result of speculation, and the profit-limit of the transport undertakings. How difficult it is to break through these multiple rings can still be seen in numerous towns and cities today, despite the fact that these various boundaries have long ago become obsolete.

The idea of the circular road—in its old significance— seemed especially useful to nineteenth-century city planners, because the railway stations could be placed on this peripheral line. But gradually the towns extended beyond this ring; the whole system became more or less meaningless, and in the end an obstacle to free development.

That administrative boundaries can be a great hindrance is well known. The problem has been demonstrated in the incorporation of numerous outer communities in the metropolitan areas of Greater London, Greater New York, Greater Paris, Greater Berlin, Greater Tokyo, and in many other cases. The consequence of delay in administrative unification almost everywhere was that speculators undertook their own private "extension of the city" beyond the area of the mother city, and mostly under more favorable conditions of taxation.

These new colonies and the people they attracted thus contributed not only to the growth of the conurbation but also to its haphazard development. The radial lines of fast traffic pierce these various rings, but limits are imposed on them by traffic policy and by the time required for the journey. Thus the problem of space develops into a problem of time.

City planning in the last decades before World War II showed more and more a preference for the radial scheme, in order to bring some order into this concentric growth of the cities. The most important means for this were green wedges extending from the green belt into the town, and radial lines of communication. The extension of the built-up areas at first followed these traffic radii, and only later was the space between them filled with buildings. However, this procedure does not get down to the roots of the problem; it does not suffice to bring order into the chaos of the urban structure. Into this general city plan secondary schemes are inserted for the layout of the different districts.

Their main elements are rectangular blocks, diagonal and radial streets; all of them are used in an unimaginative manner. Each suburb develops a "metropolitan" plan of its own.

Center and Periphery.   Centrifugal forces break up the center and strengthen the periphery. But at the same time they exert a similar influence on the separate districts. If we look at this development we see that ring-shaped zones are again spreading around the center. Each zone tends to grow at the cost of the one next within it. And in each zone both centrifugal and centripetal forces are at work. The center expands and takes over functions which were formerly fulfilled by other zones. The intermediate zones take over functions from the center and also fulfill new ones.

The same process takes place in the outer ring. Functions of work—a shifting of industry to the outskirts and along the radial lines of traffic, and concentration of commerce in the center—and functions of housing—mostly of a centrifugal nature—are the foremost influences which give each different zone its specific character. This general fluctuation and the dynamics of life make extraordinary demands on the city-planning scheme, the most essential of which is flexibility. But this is just what it hardly ever possesses.

Rigidity dominates the whole plan, for it still belongs to the period when city planning was statically conceived. The multitude of divergent forces sets everything in motion and transforms the previously small central square of the town into a central zone. The more centralized the structure of society, the more full of meaning and the more perfect is the architectural appearance of the center. If the social structure becomes more decentralized, the center of the city also loses in powerful expression, until the spread of indifference and uncertainty that is today moving over our whole civilization levels it down into a confused central zone. Within such a zone there is no longer one building or group of buildings that symbolizes the central ideas of the time, but a multitude of buildings for very different purposes.

We are living today in cities which have neither center nor limits, cities whose central zone symbolizes the power of money. The city of the masses is just as amorphous as the masses themselves. The power of money is the fictitious center—the City of London, Wall Street in New York, the Banque de France in Paris—while the residential and industrial zones surrounding this center house the modern "slaves" who are governed by this new despotic force. It is the old game of ruler and ruled, but with other symbols.

In the course of thousands of years the old centers have disappeared—the centers represented by the palaces of the autocratic kings of Egypt and Babylon; the *agora* and the temple of the democratic and self-governing citizen of the *polis;* the forum and Palatine, the twofold symbol of imperial Rome; the cathedral, the castle, the guildhalls and the town hall, symbols of the authority of the medieval towns and their craftsmen-burghers. The perspective "center" of the palace of the deified king and of the pompous festival halls in honor of God, the churches of the Baroque have also lost their dominating significance.

With all these centers went the fixed city boundaries within which human beings lived as forced settlers under the Egyptian and Babylonian kings, as free members of a community in Greece, as citizens in the Roman Empire or as subjects under the *Roi Soleil.* All these have gone today, and with them all the symbols which dominated the city. The money power alone has outlasted palace, church, and town hall, and streams along even the narrowest channels through all the city. It is not a symbol that can be accepted as representative of a really creative society.

Block, Street, and House. The built-up block is in essence nothing but the land left between the streets, which many city planners still consider as the primary element of the layout. But all three elements—blocks, streets, and houses—are equal in importance; they form a coherent whole, and none of them can be reduced to a minor position without a detrimental effect on the others. It is obviously impossible to expect satisfactory results if the idea prevails that putting together a large number of blocks of similar shape can produce a layout that will efficiently fulfill its purpose. The deplorable consequences of this misunderstanding are only too well known.

The model for many of the city-planning schemes of the second half of the nineteenth century was Haussmann's plan for Paris. This plan made no distinction between residential and traffic streets. It was a beautiful ornament consisting of straight lines converging on certain points. It was the prototype of a drawing-board pattern. The streets are everything, the houses mere by-products. Walking through the streets of Paris one gets the impression that everything—houses, cafés, shops, and people—exists only for the streets; that everything is kept in uninterrupted motion. Movement is an end in itself. Squares are circular traffic roads. However, the wide straight avenues are useful, not only as traffic arteries but also as target-lines if it should ever be necessary to hold the masses in check with guns. The *Place de la République*—from which radiate seven streets running through quarters with numerous small flats—is dominated by a barracks. The whole system is a kind of revival of the *piazza d'armi* of the Rennaissance.

There is no reason to be still enthusiastic today about the "grandiose" performance of Haussmann. He not only put the Emperor's finances on a healthy basis but provided ample opportunities of enrichment to a corrupt and parvenu society that did nothing to improve the housing standard of the masses. Their accommodation remained a negligible quantity. The far more valuable counterpart of this urban and financial "improvement" is Balzac's *Comédie Humaine,* which represents the period with much greater and deeper understanding. It is the senseless overvaluation and childish imitation of Haussmann's work to which we should object. For his own day, with its outspoken inclination for the pompous and its misunderstood rationalism, Haussmann's plans were doubtless impressive enough. But we can hardly say they had the qualities necessary to survive their time.

The separation of home from place of work influences not only the general structure of the town, but also the individual dwelling. In former periods the craftsman lived and worked in the same house, and the citizen also had his store or office attached to his private rooms. The floor-space could consequently be reduced when the work-space had been separated off, all the more because the new household was run quite differently from the old. Home production has almost completely disappeared; the storing of food and other necessities has been reduced to a minimum, as they can be bought from day to day. These factors have altered both city and house considerably, although not so much as they should have.

To compare the housing conditions in our cities with those of Rome is almost a commonplace. However, it may

be pertinent to quote a few sentences from Oswald Spengler's
The Decline of the West:

To me it is a symbol of the first importance that in the Rome of
Crassus—triumvir and all-powerful building-site speculator—the
Roman people with its proud inscriptions . . . lived in appalling
misery in the many storied lodging-houses of dark suburbs; . . .
that, while along the Appian Way there arose the splendid and
still wonderful tombs of the financial magnates, the corpses of the
people were thrown along with animal carcases and town refuse
into a monstrous common grave. In Rome and Byzantium, lodg-
ing houses of six to ten stories (with street-widths of ten feet at
most!) were built without any sort of official supervision, and frequently collapsed with all their inmates. A great part of the *cives
Romani* for whom *panem et circenses* constituted all existence,
possessed no more than a high priced sleeping-berth in one of
the swarming ant-hills called *insulae.*

Open Spaces. The value of the open spaces in a city
is determined by their distribution over the urban area.
Merely to intersperse them like oases does not enable them
to fulfill the purpose of ventilating the city and serving as
playing fields and recreation grounds for the population.
These green islands must be interrelated so that they form a
coherent park system. The path toward our present solution
begins in the Middle Ages with the private gardens, fields,
vineyards, and the cultivated land of the monasteries within
the walls of the town. It leads on to the palace gardens of the
Baroque, and to the public parks of the nineteenth century.
The garden of the medieval house was a kitchen garden
rather than a place for pleasure and recreation. The Renaissance garden was laid out in a strictly geometrical relation
to the house; its arrangement was essentially a putting together of individual motifs. The Netherlands led the way to

a more intimate adaptation between Nature and man's work. Amsterdam's tree-lined streets along the banks of the canals are the best known example. The Baroque garden was an architectural landscape in clear contrast with surrounding Nature. The English garden is a kind of domesticated Nature; it is, as it were, Nature after she has been to a public school. The average European garden of today is a characterless thing. It may contain many varieties of beautiful plants and flowers and trees, but it cannot be compared to a Chinese or Japanese garden, with its subtle selection of vegetation forming a little world of its own.

All these institutions conformed to the small scale of the towns. Large and metropolitan cities call for a different solution. The introduction of natural vegetation on a large scale to the interior of cities would split up the rigid conformation of houses to streets, and the long and sterile rows of buildings. It would bring life, change, and vigor direct to the townsman. It is no overstatement to say that this "deurbanization" of the city is the most potent instrument for turning its development into new channels and fundamentally altering its appearance.

A regeneration of the towns on the old lines is impossible. We cannot go back. But neither can we go forward in the same direction, for the revaluation of all values is a fact. The rise of the masses may lead to a catastrophe. Success can be expected only if man's personal life gains ascendancy over the forces of his functional life. The worship of quantity and of old values must give place to the creative energies inherent in an appreciation of quality and of the future. History should teach us that only a freedom which grows within limitations is formative, and that *laissez faire* leads merely to a shapeless muddle.

Under such conditions it is inevitable that the relationship between houses and streets, as the main elements in the planning of our cities, is almost the opposite of what it should be. Neither streets nor houses fulfill efficiently their specific purposes. The clear distinction between their different and even contrasting functions has been lost in a general vagueness. It is our task to plan systematically their purposive adaptation to the changing needs of the present and the future.

To balance the four functions of housing, work, recreation, and distribution, to restore the primacy of personal over functional life, to make our cities places of inspiration, beauty, and purposiveness, to harmonize the works of nature and man—this is the deeper meaning behind this transformation. The change must be drastic if our cities are to be life-centered and not traffic-centered. The way from the early beginnings of the building of urban communities is a long one. It leads, as far as European civilization is concerned, from the *polis,* with its narrow streets resembling an interspace cut out of the mass of the houses, to the military rigidity of the Roman layout; to the functional clarity of the medieval streets and their intimate adaptation to the houses. It leads in the Renaissance to the ruthless subordination of the houses to considerations of defense, which are often nothing more than a toying with geometrical forms and numbers, to the perspective view of the Baroque with the emerging Cult of the Street and to the feeble ostentatiousness of a Haussmann with his *points de vue* complex and his hypocritical façades hiding the ugliness of the houses behind them, till it ends in the chaotic mess of our present cities and the almost totalitarian primacy of nondescript streets over cut-to-pattern houses. Since the end of the Middle Ages there has been a steady decline, and since a further deterioration is hardly possible, we may hope that the way will again turn upwards.

The precarious situation of the cities in our time has been vividly and clairvoyantly described by Rainer Maria Rilke in the *Book of Hours*.[5]

> The cities, though, want only what will speed them,
> and drag all with them on their headlong course.
> They smash the beasts like rotten wood to feed them
> and use whole nations up without remorse.
>
> Their people serve some culture's domination
> and fall afar from measure and from poise,
> and give the name of progress to gyration,
> and travel with a growing acceleration,
> and have a harlot's soul and scintillation,
> and louder rings their glass and metal noise.
>
> Some phantom seems to lure them every hour,
> they can no longer be themselves at all;
> their money grows, engrosses all their power,
> and swells to east wind size, and they are small
> and vacuous and wait there for the call
> of wine and every poisonous distillation
> to rouse them to some transient occupation.

5. From *Selected Works of Rainer Maria Rilke: Volume II, Poetry*, translated by J. B. Leishman. Translation © 1960 by the Hogarth Press Ltd. Reprinted by permission of New Directions, Publishers.

chapter two

THE EXPANDING

ENVIRONMENT

"The new mentality is more important
even than the new science and the new
technology."—A. N. WHITEHEAD.

THE preceding chapter has outlined the perennial revolution through which the interaction of man and
nature has passed, shaping and reshaping the face of the
earth and the scope and character of man's activities. It has
described the historical development of cities and the mentality that transformed their physical layout, appearance,
and social structure. But it has also shown that during the
past five millennia cities remained fundamentally the same,
compact organizations within a limited compass—containers,
as Lewis Mumford has called them.

Only in the past three or four generations has this compact and limited mold been disintegrating, giving way to an

amorphous and undirected development that threatens to result in a chaotic deterioration of urban existence. If we read the signs of the historical growth of cities correctly, and if we interpret the change from an I-Thou to an I-It relationship in the interaction of man and environment, it is obvious that we have reached one of the rare turning points in the development of man.

Cities as we have known them in the past cannot survive. Something new has to be worked out, or we will never be able to break through the stifling atmosphere of stale and narrow ideas that has prevented us from adapting our environment to the great possibilities of the future.

City planning has been the eternal laggard. Now it has degenerated into inefficient and schizophrenic efforts to save the time-honored notion of urban life and urban structure. We try to combine the most modern possibilities and means —communications, traffic, public services, and industries— with traditional concepts and traditional solutions. This has created an explosive situation, an eruptive contrast between what could be and what has been. This dichotomy is irreconcilable, and it will remain so if we refuse to discard the old notion of the attraction of a city center, which has lost its intrinsic meaning, or to see cities as what they are in reality: a confused mass of unrelated details, sprawling over at the periphery into subtopias and beyond into vast conurbations.

It seems that we cannot extricate ourselves from this dilemma and attune our thinking and acting to the world that is emerging with irresistible force. The fashionable panacea is "urban renewal." But is this a remedy? It still relies on the old pattern of cities, slightly improved in detail, but hopelessly lagging behind what it could be. Let me quote from an excellent and stimulating symposium arranged by the Architectural Press of London in 1960:

Yet most citizens—including those called upon to plan—are determined to have the best of both worlds. They expect to be able to drive straight down an autoroute de l'Ouest, straight through the Arc de Triomphe, and into a Champs Elysées that still has the urbanity of a sequence from *Gigi*. They demand suburban expansiveness, and urban compactness, ancient monuments and tomorrow's mechanical aids simultaneously and in the same place. They get neither, because on one side is a tradition which cannot be expanded to deal with new developments without disintegrating, and on the other hand a disorderly pressure of new developments whose effect—because they are competitive and lack an integrating discipline—is disruptive anyhow.

Moreover, another problem is looming large on the horizon: the population explosion. If cities are "improved" through urban renewal, they will attract more people. The new millions have to be housed somewhere. If they go to the "improved" cities in large numbers because they have no other place to go to, the old vicious circle begins again and city renewal will become anew city deterioration. City renewal, if it is not made part and parcel of a comprehensive reorganization of the whole structure of settlement on a large scale, is a phantasmagoria, and in spite of the good intentions of its promoters will remain an opiate for the masses and a self-deception of those who are responsible for this flight of fancy.

Architecture and city planning are undergoing a revolution more profound than any in the past. This revolution may be less obvious in the reshaping of our cities, for urban development, and all that it implies, have always lagged behind the sometimes tempestuous changes that have taken place in architecture, although both are fundamentally one, differing only in scale. The language of form and the primary tasks are the same: the creation of space and space relations; the separation of the architectural and social space from the frightening infinity of universal space; and the physical expression of these results in a contemporary style.

City planning, working with larger units and impeded by more practical difficulties than architecture, has always been slower in its adaptation to the changing demands of new ideas and aspirations. Its time scale is more sedate, more majestic, although after a time it merges as an integral and legitimate part into the general spirit of the period. Our period is no exception. We have a considerable number of buildings that try to express—so far it is but an uncertain, groping advance which might lead into the right direction— the new concept of space and a new way of life, but there is hardly a single city or town in any country that could even faintly compete with the architectural revolution, however vague the ultimate goal of that revolution may still be.

Why, apart from the reasons of a practical sort just mentioned, is this so? I believe that the greatest difficulty we have to face is our innate reluctance to abandon the millennia-old concept of cities, of their physical appearance and layout, and of city life in general. We stubbornly refuse to admit that there might be other possibilities, that after the first five thousand years that cities have existed no fundamental changes are discernible, and that the new scale and new ideas of space wrought by our great achievements in science and technology demand an equivalent realization in our own manmade environment.

The character and form of living together, of concentration or dispersal of commodities, are among the most expressive and essential elements of the revolution of environment. The aim of the present work is to investigate these emerging trends against the background of the changes in the past. Its principal thesis is the notion of a centerless region as the next phase in the evolution of environmental structure.

I am aware that this notion may encounter considerable opposition and evoke the wrath of many planning experts. This is no reason, however, to abandon the search for a radical solution of the problems inherent in the moral and physical disintegration that threatens all cities in all countries. I am inclined to believe that this statement may be accepted as a basis and as a starting point for the following argument, and that there is at least a certain consensus of opinion, although numerous well-meaning and sincere experts and laymen will reject even this assumption. They are convinced that the basic fabric of our cities cannot be changed and that redevelopment schemes and reforms will rejuvenate our urban environment.

In this part I have tried to show a way out of this dilemma. Our present attitude towards the reshaping of our environment has led us into an impasse, and new ideas are urgently needed. These new ideas should be worked out in accordance with the revolution of environment through which we are now passing, and in the full understanding that nothing exists in isolation. It would be foolish to suggest that the far-reaching changes outlined in this work could be carried out in the span of one generation. However, it is perfectly feasible to chart the direction in which we should be moving, and to act accordingly. This is the only wise course, the only way out of the chaos, and the only hope to escape from the slothful acceptance of allegedly unalterable conditions.

A few criticisms may usefully be mentioned at the outset because they constantly preoccupy those who put their faith in a so-called "realistic approach" and discard radical solutions as meaningless. Motivating this attitude is the distrust of ideas as more potent forces than material needs and achievements, the dislike of what its proponents term 'idealism," and the overvaluation of pragmatism. It is useless to try to convince these realists, for their convictions are sincere and deep-rooted. We have to accept the existence of two opposing camps as a fact, the more so as this antagonism has existed throughout history and represents two diametrically conflicting character traits of mankind.

But there are times when one of these trends gains ascendancy over the other. Today, we are in such a period. In spite of the fact that we are witnessing today something like the ultimate fulfillment of man's fondest dreams through the twin agency of pragmatism and analysis, it seems that the primacy of ideas and synthesis is gaining momentum and that mankind is beginning to understand that ideas are the real force motivating our actions.

Possibly the most symptomatic expression of this change is the revolt against the blind overestimation of the "Expert." This revolt should not be dismissed as a passing and superficial antipathy, because science threatens to overwhelm our life and destroy our very existence. The causes are much more complex and more fundamental. Let me quote again Whitehead's words: "The new mentality is more important even than the new science and the new technology."

It is this new mentality, this emergence of ideas as the greatest formative power, that we must embrace, if we want to create a new world out of the raw materials of existence. Both the realists and the idealists can share equally in this adventure. But the realists must understand that ideas are not thin air, "such stuff as dreams are made on"; and the idealists will have to adapt the actual possibilities to their ideas, and not their ideas to expedient solutions.

Another criticism of the concept of a centerless region is the assumption that a viable economy and creative intellectual and artistic activities cannot exist without a certain concentration of energies and a cross-fertilization of minds, heretofore found only in cities. I do not deny the validity of this argument per se. However, it is based on two suppositions, neither of which is unalterable.

First, the assumption that certain achievements were dependent on close proximity in the past is no proof that this should be so in the future. Up to the present day the urban half of mankind has lived in cities which have remained essentially the same for thousands of years. Thus, gregariousness was equated to proximity, and greatness to bigness. All contemporary cities are essentially small towns that have grown amorphously on old ground plans, retaining their original small scale in detail without adapting it to totally different conditions in general. Thus, virtually all creative activities, whether economic, intellectual, or artistic, have remained concentrated in cities.

The second assumption is the result of the failure to recognize mobility as a formative factor in the revolution of environment. The scale of all our activities has broadened, or, in other words, distances are relative or even meaningless. What would have been a fatiguing journey over a long distance a generation ago is for us nothing unusual, a daily life routine. Consequently, the old notion of proximity has lost its meaning.

Economic and intellectual creativity depends, to be sure,

on cooperation and mutually fructifying exchanges. These prerequisites will continue to exist in a centerless region, with its looser and more dispersed structure of settlement. What has changed is merely the scale, that is, the larger space within which these activities are carried on, not less but more effectively, in accordance with our greatly increased mobility.

Today, the advantages of this potential mobility cannot materialize. The concentration of activities within too small a space, in our cities, has overreached itself. The automobile has become an anomaly. But instead of condemning this agent of mobility, which in any case is a rather sterile reaction, and instead of making ineffective attempts to regulate traffic, it would be far more useful to go to the roots of the problem, to the antiquated structure of our urban environment, and to concentrate all our energies on adapting it to modern conditions.

This book is, by its very nature, abstract, at least in some respects. This is unavoidable, since it deals with problems of the future and, at the same time, tries to interpret and offer an insight into the changing ideas that have been and still are operative in the perennial transformation of our environment. It is difficult to understand why most people begin to feel uneasy whenever they are asked to follow a philosophical statement that is necessarily based on abstract reasoning. But this uneasiness may not be particularly characteristic of our time alone. Goethe seems to have encountered similar reservations, for he complained more than once that "those who are afraid of ideas in the end lose their meaning."

In the following chapters I have tried to corroborate, as far as possible, the process of abstract reasoning, the impact of ideas upon city development, with concrete examples.

The first chapter forms the foundation on which the proposals for the future are based. The final goal, the centerless region in which numerous small communities joined together in a densely knit social and economic structure organically serve the innumerable functions of daily life, is, in my opinion, the logical and inevitable result of everything that has gone before. It is the natural result of the widening scale, of the breakthrough into the vast realm of new ideas and possibilities, and of the imperative need to attune our environment to these new conditions and free it from the fetters of outworn restrictions and habits.

Cities do not exist in a physical and spiritual vacuum. They do not just "happen" as historical incidents or products of human likes and dislikes. This is possibly less a truism than it may appear, for it means that cities are immensely complex symbols of the universal order. This again may seem to be an obvious truth, but I doubt that even those who would most readily agree to it are aware of its full implications, namely that man's changing ideas of space and of the universe are directly reflected in the planning of cities throughout history. Unconsciously and consciously they have shaped and reshaped cities in all lands and at all times, and thus related them to the general scheme of things. As Alexander Pope said:

"All are but part of a tremendous whole"

and

"Remember, Man, the Universal Cause
acts not by partial but by gen'ral laws."

This is the meaning, perhaps not always obvious, of the statement that cities do not exist in a void. And this is why, on the following pages, the reader's attention has been drawn to our present concept of the universe. Only if we try to fathom the tremendous changes that our ideas of the universe have undergone in the past, and the great audacity of our present concept, can we hope to understand what the new scale and the new space mean for the reshaping of our terrestrial environment, of which cities—or what may replace them—are an integral part.

Thus, the following remarks by Sir James Jeans are of vital importance. His words provide the framework for a new approach to the remaking of our cities. Our response to this great challenge will determine whether future generations will bless or condemn us. The reshaping of our environment is a moral obligation, and the highest moral standards should be our sole yardstick.

In his book *Eos, or The Wider Aspects of Cosmology,* Sir James Jeans tells us:

. . . looked at on the astronomical time-scale, humanity is at the very beginning of its existence—a new-born babe, with all the unexplored potentialities of babyhood; and until the last few moments its interest has been centred, absolutely and exclusively, on its cradle and feeding-bottle. It has just become conscious of the vast world existing outside itself and its cradle. It is learning to focus its eyes on distant objects, and its awakening brain is beginning to wonder, in a vague, dreamy way, what they are and what purpose they serve. Taking a very gloomy view of the future of the human race, let us suppose that it can only expect to survive for two thousand million years longer, a period about equal to the past age of the earth. Then, regarded as being destined to live for three-score years and ten, humanity, although it has been born in a house seventy years old, is itself only three days old. But only in the last few minutes has it become conscious that the whole world does not centre round the cradle and its trappings, and only in the last few ticks of the clock has any adequate conception of the size of the external world dawned upon it.

Even if one does not take this statement literally, it raises a number of complex problems. I believe it is fundamentally true even in its practical applications. It refers to the age of mankind as a whole, to the whole tribe of men in all parts of our planet. As social beings we are like babes; as individuals we may be a bit older, but we are by no means as mature as we flatter ourselves to be.

We are moving out of the dreamworld of our babyhood, overwhelmed by the nascent knowledge that the world is one and that everything is related in one way or another to everything else. Reluctantly do we accept new truths, new perspectives, and new surroundings; in short, everything that has not been instilled in us since our earliest days. We are fighting for institutions which in the past played the role of parental guides. We are first seeing details, and are frightened by their immediacy and deceptive magnitude, just as a baby sees only the toy before its eyes, that one toy which animates its great-little world of wavering phantoms and fleeting perceptions and eliminates, like a magnifying glass, all other phenomena.

The child and its toy—its isolated toy: this seems to be the true picture of our present transitory state. We rely on only what we can touch or directly perceive and what stimulates us immediately or is within our mental reach. But now we are forced out of our self-centered attitude, out of the world of familiar and dreamlike unrealities into the acceptance of a newly discovered universe. Of some ten thousand generations that separate us from our simian ancestors, only the last ten have begun to perceive the universe as something other than a geocentric and finite phenomenon. What, after all, are ten generations for this overwhelming change? It is only natural that mankind has not yet adapted itself to this radical revolution in thinking and acting. According to Sir James,

in any case our three-days-old infant cannot be very confident of any interpretation it puts on a universe which it only discovered a minute or two ago. . . . It has before it time enough and to spare, in which it may understand everything . . . and ever the old question obtrudes itself as to whether the infant has any means of knowing that it is not dreaming all the time. The picture it sees may be merely a creation of its own mind, in which nothing really exists except itself; the universe which we study with such care may be a dream and we brain-cells in the mind of the dreamer.

Our physical environment, our cities and towns, and our social and economic institutions all bear the mark of obsolescence. They are shallow and hollow. And yet these institutions linger on as laws and statutes, as accepted rules of behavior and standards of morality. New environmental conditions can develop only out of a new attitude towards life in its wholeness. The old forces that have shaped our environment as we know it have lost their formative power, and the most momentous of the agencies that have given idea and form in the past to our cities and buildings are also those which are in an advanced state of decline. They are the Church, the State, and Tradition. For millions this trinity was, and still is, the extreme limit of their spiritual aspirations, their earthly ambitions, and their intellectual and emotional advance. These protective shells are now threatened by the impact of new forces from within and without. From creative ideas and high ideals they have degenerated into idols, and finally into institutionalized habits.

The Church, the State, and Tradition have been the great patrons and fountainheads of art. Cities have developed around the nucleus of a church or a bishop's palace. They were founded by territorial lords or kings in the interest of the State and as symbols of its power. Tradition, at times retarding and at other times stimulating, has created a mold in which cities stagnated or developed. This era is now drawing to a close. A world is disappearing with all its old wonders and the reassuring "inertia of custom."

We are alone in a new world we cannot understand, whose frightening complexity we are just beginning to explore. The decisive factor in this process of dissolution and transition is the relationship of man to the universe, which has undergone profound changes during the last five hundred years. In the Middle Ages the *ego*, the self, was the starting point of a religious interpretation of the universe.

Pico della Mirandola expressed this conviction towards the end of the fifteenth century in the wonderful words that the Creator addresses to Adam:

In the middle of the world have I placed thee that thou mayst the more easily look about thee and see all that is therein contained. Thou canst degenerate into the beast or reshape thyself into a godlike being. Thou alone hast the power of development, of growth according to free will. Thou hast the germ of an all-embracing life in thee.

These thoughts are like a bridge spanning the abyss that had opened between the narrow world of medieval life enclosed by the shells of the family, the guilds, the fraternities, the city walls, and the concentric spheres of the universe arranged around the earth, and the outward explosion of the Renaissance that burst asunder the old limitations and gave men a sun-centered universe terminating in the sphere of the fixed stars.

Man and earth were removed from the center, and a new interpretation of the universe and of man's place in it became possible. For a genius of the Baroque, for Rembrandt, this led to an awe-inspiring feeling of loneliness in the face of eternity. His human beings stand between emptiness and infinity. Modern man was born, and with him all the problems that in our time threaten to engulf us in a welter of diffidence and in the search for an answer to the mysteries of the universe and the terrestrial environment.

A similar dilemma and doubt pervade the relationship of the citizens to the State. As long as the unit of the State, or for that matter of a tribe, a city-state, or a town, was small in scale and dense in structure, as long as State and Community were one, architecture and the design and building of cities grew out of a cultural unity of everyday life and a spontaneous certainty that were ever present and never artificial. But as soon as State and Community began to fall apart, the decline of spontaneous creativeness set in, until it disappeared under the impact of the impersonal forces of a State that had become a vague unreality and could not be experienced directly.

The old taboos, which in the past guaranteed social coherence and economic rationality in accordance with a particular stage of development, are still alive today. We drag them along like chains that fetter our individuality and retard a cultural revival. Let us revert for a moment to Sir

James Jeans' suggestion that we are still very young, still living in our cradle or perhaps just beginning to move about in our play-pen and to try to stand erect by holding fast to its railings. It is precisely this intermediate stage between the utmost dependence on others and the very beginning of independence and individual movements that is characteristic of our relation to the State.

But modern man is in a particularly serious predicament. The power and demands of the State are growing stronger from day to day, and the time seems not too far off when we will have to decide whether the State exists for us or we for the State. This is a crucial choice which will have repercussions in all fields of existence, not least in city planning and architecture.

Two antagonistic attitudes are visible today. There are the eternal conformists, who are ready to accept the ascendancy of the State as an unavoidable fact, and consequently will listen to even the most superficial slogans with which a superficial propaganda tries to dull their independent judgment. But there are also those who are conscious of their own individuality and refuse to be lulled into the security of an easy conformity. These eternal rebels against the leveling embrace of group bondage under the cover of patriotism, nationalism, professional interests, and the like are ready to rely on their own responsibility and their own strength. The State, as we know it today and as it seems to be developing, has practically abdicated its role as a creative agent of city planning.

The era is ending that saw the State play an active role in the foundation and growth of cities. There is a long line of development from the early and rudimentary beginnings of the national State: from the kingdoms of Egypt and Babylon, resembling royal domains, to the Greek city-states, with their deliberately limited size, to the clearly defined entities of the cities and towns of the Roman Empire; to the small-scale towns of the Middle Ages, the narrow and yet eventful world of the burghers. It leads in the Renaissance to the small principalities vying for the primacy of cultural perfection, and in the Baroque to the rise of national states with their identification of king and State, to the *l'état c'est moi* doctrine, until it ends in the uncreative state of modern times, with its ambiguous pretentions and its almost complete abdication in the sphere of city planning.

True, in some countries the State has taken a certain interest in city development, as, for instance, in England or the U.S.S.R. But these activities can hardly be compared to the great achievements of the past. They are more or less restricted to financial support, a few administrative remedies, and other minor alleviations. The cities and towns have been thrown back upon their own initiative and the competition between them makes schemes on a regional scale impossible.

The third factor that has exerted a great influence on the origin and growth of cities is tradition. There is a tradition in depth and a tradition of the surface, two aspects of the same problem that are more or less synonymous with subconscious and conscious tradition, respectively. The former is like a never-ending thread twisted together with the innumerable fibers of our being, reaching down to its deepest layers. The latter resembles a tapestry, woven of the narratives of recorded events of the past, hung on the walls of the narrow passage through which life proceeds.

Without those memories of the past, the walls would be bare to the eyes of the many who feel lost in a world that grows from day to day more impersonal and estranged from the asylum of cherished habits and customs. But now this tradition of surface values is rapidly disintegrating. Like a museum, it offers a marvelous collection of interesting achievements of the past, which only very few visitors understand in their deeper meaning and in their significance for the personal life of past generations. But the majority of people, and not least those who are responsible for the welfare of our cities, insist on the convenient belief that history repeats itself and that for this reason tradition is an indispensable stimulus of all our actions.

Just the opposite is true. History never repeats itself. There are only superficially similar situations that appear to be similar if they are taken out of the configuration as a whole. Were this not so, life would not be worth living, for it would mean that mankind is an unchangeable entity moving within the same narrowly limited orbit and just marking time. The tradition of the surface, the repetition and the preservation of external forms, is sheer escapism. It is the expression of diffidence and of our longing for a reassurance against the uniqueness of our situation. It is a retroactive affirmation for our conformity, with the usual standards of behavior recognized and sanctioned by history, which we tend to read as a reversed utopia, as the Golden Past, as if it were an inspiring leader into the future.

Let there be no mistake about it. Today, the danger of cultural stagnation is very great and the forces of sterile tradition are very strong. In city planning they shield themselves behind the excuse that far-reaching changes cannot be made, nor even envisaged, because practical considerations have to be given first priority. Unfortunately, the lies and propaganda of our period, when words have lost their meaning and art has become a tool of political expediency, have spread to the sphere of city planning, obscuring the very essence of this most social of all the arts and almost completely obliterating its profoundly human character.

And yet the first tremors of opposition against this complacent timidity can be felt. The soothing words of official city planners are listened to with growing scepticism. New ideas begin to find more acceptance, and more and more people are aware that a new order of things is in the making, that a new order of things is born, demanding a radical break with the past and new forms of urban life. Before we set out to conquer the moon or to visit other planets, it may not be too inappropriate to remind those who indulge in a spending orgy of fantastic dimensions that there is still something to be done on our old planet, the earth.

The urge of mankind to explore the vast spaces of the universe cannot be stopped. It is too deeply rooted in human nature. It is the most cherished symbol of our time to explore, to expand, to conquer, and to reach for what only a generation ago appeared impossible. This outburst of creative energies, which unfortunately has degenerated into a war of national propaganda, should remind us that we are capable of overcoming our inertia and modesty, if we want it and if we understand that there are, in every country, two civilizations fighting for supremacy: the forces of chaos, multiplying the chaos with their shortsightedness and folly, and the forces of wisdom, order, and insight into the complex nature of the emerging changes and possibilities of a united world.

It is a disappointing picture, and yet it contains the germ of hope and final success, a promise upon which we may reflect with sadness but also with wonder, for the frontiers of what is possible have been moved far beyond our wildest dreams and beyond the line of least resistance. Why cannot this new sense of possibility be given an outlet in a revolution of environment on earth that would rejuvenate our existence and our cities and regions? There can be no doubt that it can be done, if the time-honored slogans and evasions are brushed aside and recognized as what they are in reality, as the rearguard battle of timid conformists, of insincere politicians and profiteers.

Let us return to our three-day-old babe. It has just realized that it is not the center of the universe. It is still frightened because it cannot put a sensible interpretation to the outside world that begins to emerge from the mist of its dreams in ever clearer shapes and with ever greater immediateness. It is not only the growing pressure of a shrinking world that is closing in upon mankind and creating a feeling of timidity and confusion, but the multitude of new possibilities and the apparent helplessness in coordinating the innumerable details and unforeseen problems that assail man from all sides.

Only the last ten generations have viewed "the problem of their existence in anything like its proper astronomical perspective," as Sir James Jeans puts it. For all the others the universe was a static and limited entity with the earth as the center. Ten generations is nothing on the astronomical time scale and not even very much in relation to known history. Our universe is in a dynamic equilibrium and infinite. As the early exponent of this new concept, Giordano Bruno, said in *Cena de la Ceneri:* "the world is infinite. Therefore, there is no body that can be said to be in the center of the world." To this infinite world man must attune himself.

Many people will object that "the goings-on of the universe" are not their concern, and that in any case they have no connection whatever with their daily thoughts and activities. This is another of the numerous illusions that prevent us from seeing things whole and from adapting our environment to a new scale in time and space. People may be more inclined to accept this self-evident truth if their doubts are soothed by the retrospective sedative of time and tradition.

One example may be sufficient. For the Egyptians, the universe was static, and correspondingly their own world was changeless. This concept influenced their whole life, their attitude to the State, their religion, and all their works of art. As Professor Frankfort says in *Ancient Egyptian Religion*, with reference to the pyramids: "they express, with unanswerable finality, the ancient Egyptian's conviction that this universe was a world without change."

So it is today, except that our universe is totally different from that of the Egyptians. To use once more the words of Sir James Jeans in *The Mysterious Universe:*

... the universe begins to look more like a great thought than like a great machine. . . . The old dualism of mind and matter . . . seems likely to disappear, not through matter becoming in any way more shadowy or insubstantial than heretofore, or through mind becoming resolved into a function of the working of matter, but through substantial matter resolving itself into a creation and manifestation of mind. . . . A soap-bubble with irregularities and corrugations on its surface is perhaps the best representation, in terms of simple and familiar materials, of the new universe revealed to us by the theory of relativity. The universe is not the interior of the soap-bubble, but its surface and we must always remember that, while the surface of the soap-bubble has only two dimensions the universe-bubble has four—three dimensions of space and one of time. And the substance out of which this bubble is blown, the soap-film, is empty space welded on to empty time.

An epoch that has been able to create this unique concept of the universe cannot be too badly off. It must be inspired with a spirit of adventurous vision and a fearless urge to think its thoughts to the very end, to the outermost signposts of knowledge, insight, and inquiring adventure. The infinite, centerless universe has been conceived in the same spirit which is disrupting the parochial States, the old ways of planning our cities and towns and building our houses. Our present situation is like the void between two magnetic fields, between the past and the future. But we should at least begin to understand that the new scale of time and space cannot remain without repercussions in our thinking and acting on earth. The future begins today, and we are witnessing its first great achievements.

THE BURSTING
FRONTIERS

In *The Phenomenon of Man,* Père Teilhard de Chardin, one of the great thinkers and most optimistic visionaries of our age, asks: "Are we not at every instance living the experience of a universe whose immensity, by the play of our senses and our reason, is gathered up more and more simply in each one of us?" To this fateful question we have to give the answer, which cannot be anything else than in the affirmative. But we are still unprepared to accept its inescapable truth. We refuse to admit, and above all, to act accordingly, that the growth of the world's population and the improvement of human communications have destroyed the old frontiers and united our world in spirit and in reality. Père Teilhard interprets this dilemma as the result of a two-fold crisis whose onset began in earnest as early as the Neolithic age and which rose to a climax in the modern world, [deriving] in the first place from a *mass-formation* (we might call it a "planetigation") of mankind. Peoples and civilizations reached such a degree either of physical communion or economic interdependence or frontier contact that they could no longer develop save by interpenetration of one another. But it also arises out of the fact that, under the combined influence of machinery and the super-heating of thought, we are witnessing *a formidable upsurge of unused powers*. Modern man no longer knows what to do with the time and the potentialities he has unleashed. We groan under the burden of this wealth. We are haunted by the fear of "unemployment."

And he goes on pointing out the fruitlessness of settling international conflicts by a readjustment of frontiers, or of regarding as "leisure" the potential activities that are available to mankind. "Something will explode if we persist in trying to squeeze into our tumble-down huts the material and spiritual forces that are henceforward on the scale of a world."[1]

We are living in an explosive age that dissolves all frontiers—the economic, industrial, and social frontiers as well as those between states and cities, between cities and country, and between man and environment. We are told that the metropolis is exploding. We are warned of a population explosion. We are threatened by the fall-out of an atomic explosion. And those explosions are by no means all we have to cope with. There are the more subtle explosions of conformity, of mass culture and mass suggestion, of managerial efficiency and ideological generalities.

1. I am indebted to Harper & Brothers, the publishers of *The Phenomenon of Man* by Teilhard de Chardin for permission to quote the preceding sentences.

But there is one explosion more powerful than all the rest, although it is less obtrusive and sometimes almost forgotten: the explosion of Truth. Truth cannot be suppressed, at least not for a long time. It will break through the thought-barrier and finally dissolve the clouds of confusion, distrust, and meaningless verbiage that befog the mind of mankind. Let there be no mistake: these shibboleths have invaded all spheres of life, and it is for this reason that we have to deal with these problems in this particular connection, the more so as cities are one of the most complex and most misunderstood manifestations of the human spirit.

Only a few centuries ago the simple and tangible economic basis of our civilization was the soil and its subdivision. On the soil rested the nucleus of every group, be it the family, the clan, the tribe, the city-state, the city, or the State. On its size and use depended economic and social life, progress, stagnation, or retrogression. It was a religious symbol and the most realistic property a man could own. Today, all this has changed fundamentally. In many countries real estate has become a commodity whose value is controlled by the so-called Law of Supply and Demand.

The impersonal and fluctuating medium of money, the new religious symbol, with its unlimited mobility has made national frontiers, as all other frontiers, obsolete historical incidents. Only a few centuries ago, fire and human and animal power augmented by technical devices were the main energy available to man. This too has changed fundamentally. Instead of this limited and locally restricted energy we have an unlimited power supply without any geographical restrictions.

And only a few centuries ago, the bulk of the population, the inarticulate masses, was still relatively small. Its size was manageable, and its needs and aspirations were more or less comprehensible. Today, the masses have entered the stage of history in their own right. The revolt of the masses is a fact that is felt in all countries of the world, sweeping aside class distinctions and demanding a radical change in our way of living and in the institutions that can contain and direct a mass civilization.

All the transformations have created a situation where the pressure of quantitative change is turned into a qualitative revolution. And this amounts to what Père Teilhard has described in the words:

. . . life is taking a step, a decisive step, in us and in our environment. After the long maturation that has been steadily going on during the apparent immobility of the agricultural centuries, the hour has come at last, characterized by the birth pangs inevitable in another change of state.

The cause that is producing and uniting these momentous transformations is a change in our mode of thinking, more far-reaching and more potent than any change we can observe on the surface. We are beginning to be aware of the direction and of the meaning of the direction in which we are moving, moving away from a world that from our vantage-point looks relatively simple, tidily divided into more or less orderly compartments and separated by clearly defined frontiers and organized in an intelligible social hierarchy.

Can we maintain the belief that in these conditions our cities can continue to be what they have been in the past —creative agents of a revolution of environment in spirit and in fact? To ask this question is to give the answer. The old notion of cities as containers of culture and civilization is dead. The frontiers that were the *raison d'être* of these containers are dissolving before our eyes, and yet we try to retain them, hoping that improvement and renewal will adapt them to the demands of the future.

Those who put their trust in these remedies fail to understand the essence of the challenge that confronts us. What is needed is not reform but fundamental changes in our environment that are compatible with a frontierless world and with societies affluent not merely in material goods but, above all, in awareness of the intellectual and spiritual pontentiality of mankind.

The concept of potentiality is one of the most creative gifts bestowed on mankind. True, like many other notions, it has been debased and misused—as, for instance, in the political wrangles we have to suffer at the present. Diplomats and politicians, these professional expediency-mongers, use it as a welcome excuse for their unimaginative and insincere dealings, proclaiming that politics is the art of the possible.

But what is possible? Possible is what suits their own purpose. This is not the true meaning of the concept of potentiality, which is totally independent of opportunist and *ad hoc* decisions. It is a state or a quality that possesses the latent power to develop into activity, and as such it has an objective and inevitable character. As a matter of fact it is a conservative power, which continues the development latent in a situation, bringing it to the surface and making it active. Consequently, we have to observe the actual state of affairs at its termination, in its most recent manifestations, not in any of its earlier stages.

In this connection I would like to add a few sentences, quoted from an excellent article, "Tradition," by George

Boas in the Fall 1960 issue of *Diogenes*, which are very pertinent to our situation.

If our ways of living have been developed to meet needs which once were real and if they survive in part because some of these needs continue to be felt, then, when traditions are violated or set aside, it may well be because they no longer satisfy any needs. . . . [But] few things are ever lost in a society simply because they are no longer useful. . . . The importance of this is seen in the justification of our obsolete practices. . . . The moment an institution is justified on the ground that it is good-in-itself . . . it has lost its utility and is being kept alive as *objets d'art* . . . by the "inertia of custom" . . . that gives stability and hence psychological security to a society. . . . But there happen to be times when the total situation confronting an individual or a society is so novel that no precedents can be found for solutions to new problems. I should like to suggest that the middle twentieth century is one such time.

An intellectual revolution has taken place that renders our social and economic structure obsolete and reduces our cities and towns to interesting museum pieces, still encrusted with the vestiges of their neolithic past. The premachine age is still omnipresent in all our cities, and their relationship to the countryside is still the same as in the eighteenth century.

But the technical civilization has invaded this antiquated sphere with an explosive force, bursting through the material and ideal frontiers that contained urban life in the past. The essence of our technical civilization is its universality. It is not restricted to cities and towns. It engulfs all parts of a country with equal intensity and effaces the distinction between urban and rural areas. This is not to say that the country is being urbanized and the cities ruralized. But it does mean that the gulf that separated country-people and townspeople in the past is disappearing, and that the spirit of a technical civilization pervades the life of both sections of the population.

This knowledge is bound to influence our actions and to shape our decisions, whether we intend to perpetuate the old course of least resistance or to seek a dynamic solution to the new problems pressing in upon us. On the one side we have the certainty of a disastrous policy of muddling through and trying to preserve something that is already moribund, and on the other side we have a certain risk of making mistakes; but we have also the assurance that we move on stimulated by the moral obligation to create an environment that is worthy of our potentialities and of the obligation to our fellow-men. Since city planning is above all a moral activity, the choice is clear for every conscientious human being.

In order to understand the potentiality of our situation, we have to get a clear picture of its actuality, of what exists at the moment. Innumerable books have been written about the contemporary problems, and it is not my intention to add another tome to this list. In this connection it is sufficient to select some of the main trends that have a more direct bearing on city planning and to investigate in broad outline whether they tend to persist or to fade out, whether they are potentially useful or detrimental to a regenerated society, and whether they are valuable or disadvantageous to a re-shaping of our environment.

Cities are the power stations of our technical mass civilization. In these giant containers, ideas and habits, technical skills and inventions are transformed into new energy, spreading over vast areas and connected by the invisible bonds of similar pursuits and interests. The power lines and the pylons are symbolic media of this process. They herald an age of large-scale unification, without separating frontiers, and a new response to the urgent need to transform our environment and to rescue our cities and towns from their physical and social obsolescence.

The pressure of population and the pressure of conformity are most acutely felt in the cities. A semitechnical mass civilization is spreading over the globe; and with it urbanization is increasing, attracting and absorbing into its orbit ever more people. However, this statement needs qualification. That the pull of the cities and of their advantages, as imagined by the not too discriminating many, is irresistible is a fact that needs no elaboration. Whether these expectations are justified is another question. The answer depends less on the quantity than on the quality of what the masses expect and regard as ingredients of a "good life."

Without being too condescending, we may assume that material prosperity appears as a more desirable goal than intellectual advancement. A paradoxical situation is developing: while in the sphere of material affluence the common denominator of ambitions is fairly high in general, the opposite is the case when it comes to the ideal, that is, to the intellectual and cultural development of the individual person. Here the common denominator is low, for what is offered has to be adapted to the less ambitious and less gifted members of society, just as in a convoy the slowest ship determines the speed of all the others.

We may regret this, but we cannot change human nature. The ideal goods which cannot be bought or traded in for a small down-payment can only be acquired by intense mental efforts, which some people do not care to make or are constitutionally incapable of making. There are, of course, large numbers of socially and economically underprivileged people who may be capable and willing to make these efforts, but are denied the chance to do so because the society in which they live is too ill-balanced to absorb them as productive members and to offer them the means of material and intellectual advancement. This unpalatable fact is mostly glossed over by paying lip-service to the equal possibilities from which a so-called open society excludes no one.

In other countries, especially where newly won independence has revealed a disquieting lack of intellectual leaders or where social revolutions have fundamentally changed the structure of society, the need to make up for lost opportunities or to spread new ideas is accompanied by an almost ascetic attitude to material well-being. But however different the approach to these problems may be, one fact is common to all countries of the world. The tentacles of mass civilization, fully or semitechnical, have gripped all nations and are most felt in the cities. Consequently, this is one of the starting points where the concept of potentiality has to be put to the test. The cities of the present are not made for a mass civilization. They are overwhelmed by it, and the great scientific and technical possibilities they could offer cannot fully unfold.

The masses are the real sufferers of this vicious circle. They have become, more or less unknowingly, the victims of psychological mass manipulation. I do not think that we should make the "adman" the only scapegoat of our discomfiture. It is Society that is in the dock, not just one particular group. And let us not forget that some sort of mass manipulation has existed since the beginning of known history. It was exerted by the ruling minorities at all times and in all lands, either under the guise of *panem et circenses*, as in Rome, or as an appeal to civic responsibility and local patriotism, as in most periods of history; or it was enforced by the threat and use of brute force, as by the Nazis and Fascists, or by arousing religious fanaticism, as in the crusades, or by religious hysteria, as in the building of medieval cathedrals.

All these emanations of the all too human urge to win the masses for a particular purpose are not essentially different from our own methods. They differ in degree but not in principle. Our methods are more "scientific," more all-embracing, more subtle and more refined, and sometimes more intense. Though they have been perfected in the commercial field, they are also successfully applied in national and local politics, not least in shaping ideas of city development in accordance with the wishes of small and not selflessly interested minorities.

The most objectionable aspect of these activities is not the success of advertising campaigns in persuading people to buy this rather than that product, turning what could be a healthy consumers' society into an arena where the public relations experts of competing producers fight one another with the high-minded hypocrisy of witch doctors. The real ground for the strongest condemnation of these methods lies rather in their latent influence upon the emotional response of individual persons or like-minded groups of persons to the need for making decisions.

It is inevitable that this mass manipulation stereotypes and lowers the level of individual responsibility by building up "ideal" images that can easily be "bought" by anyone, if only he follows the guidance of the manipulators. But these images themselves, say of social status, of the responsible father of a family, of community members in good standing, of maternal love, can be made to materialize only if one listens to the admen and buys a new car every two years, or a deodorant or a washing machine.

These perverse associations of ideals and material goods are too well known to be scrutinized in detail. What is important is to understand that according to this mentality the ideal can be reached only through material improvement instead of through the reverse process. The disquieting feature of this ridiculous travesty is that innumerable people are taken in by this topsy-turvy appeal to human aspirations.

Some time ago a well-meaning and convinced Quaker, who happened to be a professional public relations man, told me with all the sincere indignation he was capable of: "But it is immoral to prevent a man from advertising his goods." He was at a loss to grasp the wider implications and to understand the leveling-down and the degrading reduction of the consumers' ability to make a rational choice. He thought that it was quite natural that motivation research and depth psychology are enlisted as helpers in this appeal to irrationality.

If the result of this outburst of misguided energies and pseudoscientific efforts were restricted to the consumers' market, we might be justified to ridicule it, hoping that it would die through its own inherent contradictions. But the real danger of this reliance on and appeal to irrationality is that it "conditions" millions of people to a mental inertia, a state in which they are ready to discard their own responsibility in decision-making and to submit to political and social apathy.

These indirect effects of psychological manipulation undermine the foundations of our not-too-open society. The image-salesmen are already at work, applying the methods that have been successful for selling a shaving lotion to social and political problems. Ideas have to be "put over," public figures have to be "built up," and social controversies have to be "glossed over" and "explained." Thus, an atmosphere of apathy toward almost everything that transcends the immediate needs and the direct concern of the conditioned citizen is created, and with it a state of mind that is tantamount to an abdication of personal civic responsibilities.

But we have to live in a mass society that is drawn into the whirlpool of a scientific and technical revolution. We have to try to break up the homogenized apathy of the masses by awakening their conscious selves and their inherent ability to make decisions for themselves. We must tell them what they could be, what they can get, and what potential forces are at their disposal, if they will it. The individual must be rediscovered in the masses, and apathetic conformity must be replaced by "a harmonized collectivity of consciousness," as Père Teilhard has expressed it. This is the opposite of mass manipulation. It is an opening up of new channels into which hitherto misguided or repressed energies can be directed. What is needed is, instead of apathy, sensibility; instead of credulity, inquisitiveness; instead of conformity, individuality; and instead of self-complacency, a spirit of rebellion against predigested ideas.

The results of mass manipulation are evident everywhere, perhaps in its most terrifying and most immediate aspect in the standardized subtopias, the slums of tomorrow. Who is to blame for these excesses of a laissez-faire economy, for the insincere promises of a ready-made paradise with split levels, shining kitchens, curvilinear streets, and all the paraphernalia of a status-seeking romanticism? Certainly not only the developers who have built these mass-produced homes for the *faubourgeoisie*. What they have done is exactly what our civilization deserves, and it is, above all, society that is to blame because it has allowed these nightmares to become a reality.

Words of André Gide come to mind. In *Nouvelles Nourritures* he says:

But see what Man has made of the Promised Land, a land bestowed on him as a priceless heritage. . . . I picture the dreary approaches to towns! Ugliness, discord, smell . . . And I dream of the gardens they might have been, children of understanding love; girdles of cities and guardians of the most tender and luxuriant greenness. . . . I dream too of what leisure might have been! Spiritual recreation in the benediction of joy! And work, work even, redeemed and saved from an impious curse . . . It is not only a question of changing the World, but also of changing Man. Friend, believe nothing; do not accept anything for which you have no proof. Desire for knowledge engenders doubt. End credulity. Teach yourself. Do not accept life as Men offer it to you. Rather ceaselessly persuade yourself that your life and that of others might be more beautiful; as soon as you realize that it is not God but Man who is responsible for almost all the evils of life, you will have no share in them. Do not make sacrifices to false Gods.

These false Gods, the exponents of contemporary religion, are money and material success. Their seats of power, their temples, are concentrated in the centers of cities, from which their high priests, the leaders of banking and commerce, manipulate the life of the masses. Cities of the past were built around temples and churches, palaces and town halls, as meaningful centers of society. They were small in scale, and organic entities. Today, the city centers, with their banks, insurance companies, and commercial palaces, are the strongholds of a fractional mass society, vast in scale and amorphous in structure.

The city centers of the past held the urban communities together, and their significance and their symbolic and realistic attraction was deeply rooted in the religious and political, the social and economic soil of human existence. Today, in spite of the great power that is concentrated in the city centers, these bonds have lost their uniting influence, largely because they have degenerated into purely materialistic instruments of an acquisitive and affluent society, and because their symbolic essence has evaporated into a fall-out of financial transactions.

If we try to pierce the fog of uplifting generalities that surrounds the glorification of present-day city centers, we should ask ourselves: does a city center in one of the big cities of the New World, those without a long tradition, still mean anything to the masses, even if it is rebuilt on a sumptuous scale? Can new hotels, new commercial buildings, and even a skating rink thrown into the bargain, really evoke a community feeling and arouse the interest of the masses? The answer is obvious: they cannot revive a spirit that has been fading out under the impact of a depersonalized society. Moreover, these city centers have powerful rivals in the shopping centers, where all the ingredients of a good life can be bought on a charge account. These are the new cathedrals around which the houses of the credulous citizens are clustered.

This is truer than it may appear. It seems that shopping centers are becoming the new community centers. In a few cases serious attempts have been made in this direction, and with obvious success. Shopping is almost a family ritual for old and young, and it is most likely that this trend will continue and will be exploited by the enlightened self-interest of clever business executives.

Another by-product of the quantity adoration is the pursuit of growth for growth's sake. Both these ideas are, of course, the direct outcome of a developing mass civilization whose needs are above all assessed in material terms, and both are, needless to say, intimately interconnected. The notions of quantity and growth are two almost identical aspects of the same problem, and have exerted a devastating influence on our cities and on the so-called philosophy, if there is any at all, that is behind the urban explosion.

Is there really any justification for the antiquated conviction that a big city or a metropolis has the mission to grow, and that a halt to this growth and a subsequent decrease are tantamount to decline and finally to stagnation? The cities are fighting a losing battle against the impact of new forces, against the steady influx of newcomers, against the self-defeating increase of the number of motor cars, and against an industrial system that is geared to an alleged deproletarianization of the masses.

It may be that in the so-called affluent societies of the West more and more people will share in the blessings of an urbanized and deproletarianized existence, but it is very doubtful that aid even on a large scale to underdeveloped countries could materially improve the life of the underprivileged masses in these societies, and stem the advance toward an unsystematic urbanization, repeating all the mistakes of an unplanned expansion. Are the exponents of this system, the organization men and the executive, these typical products of an urbanized society, really the *élite* of the New Age? And is it possible to readjust this system to a determined policy of survival, survival not only in a political but, above all, in a human sense, without a systematically planned revolution of environment and a massive increase in public investment?

There is now much talk going on about the need for a

new purpose, and new frontiers to be discovered and reached, but we fail to ask ourselves what this new purpose could be, and where the new frontiers are, and what to expect from this "moving ahead." In other words, we are again indulging in the comfort of slogans without investigating the situation that exists at the moment, from which the potential development must start and take its cue. Or we may say that we seem to intend to muddle through according to a non-existent plan. All this is not good enough, and it is useless to meet a novel situation with conventional reactions.

However, the masses are restless, and perhaps for the first time in the history of mankind are agitated, all over the world, by the revolutionary thought of a meaningful future that would not only improve their material well-being but above all give them an intelligible idea in which they can believe and for which they can work and live. They are tired of meaningless generalities that have been worn thin by misuse. They feel that the arrogant disregard with which they are treated by their so-called leaders is an offense to their intellect and to their justified aspirations.

They are getting increasingly sceptical of the qualifications of their representatives—for instance, of the incurable ambition of city councilors to use their ephemeral power to impose their own ignorant ideas of city planning and architecture on the city, instead of following the advice of enlightened planners and architects; or of private developers for whom personal profit is more important than public welfare.

The main concern of these petty opportunists is to satisfy the demand for standardized cells for human ants, relying on the apathetic modesty of the masses and their ignorance of what they could get, if they were better informed and less exposed to the soporific effects of psychological manipulation. The reversal of this process is a formidable task. As Sir Julian Huxley said at the Darwin Centennial Convocation of the University of Chicago in 1961:

It is hard to break through the firm framework of an accepted belief-system and to build new and complex successors, but it is necessary. It is necessary to organize our *ad hoc* ideas and scattered values into a unitive pattern transcending conflicts and divisions in its unitary web. Only by such reconciliation of opposites and disparates can our belief-systems release us from inner conflicts: only so can we gain that peaceful assurance which will help unlock our energies for development in strenuous practical actions. [The new organization of thought-belief-systems] must help us to think in terms of an overriding process of change, development, and possible improvement, to have our eyes on the future rather than on the past, to find support in the growing body of our knowledge, not in fixed dogma or ancient authority. [And he went on to stress the imperative need to free the individual from the fetters of conformity and timidity, for] our thinking must also be concerned with the individual. The well-developed, well-patterned individual human being is, in a strictly scientific sense, the highest phenomenon of which we have any knowledge; and the variety of individual personalities is the world's greatest richness.

This goal cannot be reached, if we continue to boast of "the biggest city," the "highest skyscrapers," the most beautifully landscaped shopping center, the greatest variety of commercialized entertainment; and if we follow the advice of well-meaning but shortsighted experts who tell us: let us improve our down-town areas; or if we believe enthusiastic romantics who try to persuade us that slums have a particular human appeal that should not be destroyed. What romantic misconceptions! What a lack of vision and audacity! The frontiers of the mind which have contained and preserved these outmoded notions are bursting. New vistas are opening before our eyes and new responses have to be found to the challenge of the future.

THE PRICE OF A TECHNOLOGICAL CIVILIZATION

Men are creating, not only in the West but in all parts of the world, a technological civilization, without realizing that we have to pay a very high price for every gain in the technical improvement of our environment and, above all, for the irresistible and all-embracing claim which the scientific attitude makes upon our life. This may be unavoidable, but at least it should be understood and recognized. The more scientific and technological progress pervades our thinking and acting, the more we tend to discard as unrealistic, as external and more or less superfluous "appearances," everything that cannot be touched, measured, or turned to a useful purpose, and cannot be verified and formulated into a theory and general laws.

Or, in more positive words: without our being fully aware of what is happening to us, our aesthetic and emotional sensuous qualities are becoming atrophied, and the regenerating power of aesthetic enjoyment is relegated to the sphere of mysterious irrelevancies from which it might be allowed to emerge when we have no "better" things to do, that is, when we are not engaged in practical activities. The result is a type of modern man who is so immersed in intellectual speculation and its transformation into realistic and utilitarian instruments that the immediate beauty radiating from the experience of aesthetic and emotional forces has almost totally disappeared from his life.

Most people are hardly aware of this loss of one of the most creative factors of our personalities. They do not know that they are fractional human beings, and they do not see that there is anything basically wrong in being crowded together in huge mass-produced tenements, in cities disingenuously laid out on gridiron plans, and in having to walk in canyons between walls of steel, concrete, and glass. In their own creation they are tolerated by the traffic and reduced to pygmies who cannot even admire the brutal grandeur of the buildings without craning their necks, for the streets would have to be ten times as wide to see the buildings as they actually are.

All this is not surprising. It is exactly what a confused and only half-developed technological civilization deserves. Let us hope that posterity will look at this period with a feeling of proud and justified superiority. Let us hope that it will possess enough insight to realize that only men who were overwhelmed by the dawning awareness of the limitless possibilities of science and technology could have created and connived at this framework for urban existence, and that the lack of aesthetic sensibility and emotional reactions was due to and may be excused by the dizzy and youthful enthusiasm for a new world of immeasurable technical and scientific wonders.

The attitude of fractional man to the cities is ambivalent —or more drastically put, schizophrenic. It is akin to love-hate. The inefficiency of the cities is felt though not consciously recognized. And at the same time the attraction of the cities persists, surrounded by a *mystique*, which like all similar imponderables cannot easily be defined, and by the illusion of a "better life" than in the country, with its hard labor, fewer opportunities, less variety, and the restricting rhythm of Nature that no farmer or peasant can escape.

The urbanization of the world is increasing at an alarming rate, in direct proportion to the growth of the world population. It is accelerating in underdeveloped countries, which are still predominantly agrarian and are inhabited by almost two-thirds of the world population, and it is relatively decelerating in the industrial countries of the West, where the Industrial Revolution took place five or six generations ago, and the urgent need for manpower induced millions to leave the country and settle in the cities.

On the other hand, the underdeveloped countries often have to cope with rural overpopulation—China and India are the classical examples—and living standards near the existence minimum, driving large numbers of impoverished and uprooted countrypeople to the cities, where the already saturated labor market cannnot absorb them. In these rural areas

masses of humans stagnate, even in our day, in a natural milieu with agriculture handicapped by unfavourable soil and climatic conditions, by the absence of irrigation, of fertilization, and in general, of technical equipment, and the persistence, in the cultural context, of traditional attitudes foreign (or hostile) to the productivity of labor, as well as a galloping demographic expansion, [that] does not protect them from famine.

George Friedman, the author of this article, "Re-Evaluation of Modern Societies," published in the Fall 1960 issue of *Diogenes*, then goes on explaining how

the wretchedness of the countryside, the mirages of industrializa-
tion, have impelled crowds towards the towns; São Paulo, Buenos
Aires, Johannesburg, Casablanca, Calcutta, among many other
agglomerations not prepared to absorb this influx, surround themselves with the sordid *bidonvilles* and *gourbivilles* of North
Africa, *Callampas* of Chile, *faveles* of Brazil, *bustees* of India,
shanty towns of Johannesburg, etc. to which the "models" of mass
communication and of technical civilization penetrate too quickly.
Masses, uprooted from their natural milieu and not integrated
into the new milieu of modern societies, often know, and at their
lowest level, cinema, radio, television, illustrated magazines (sex
and crime) before they know the elements of physical well-being
(housing, food, clothing) and basic education.

In 1900 there were ten cities in the world with a million
or more inhabitants. Today there are sixty-one, and two out
of every ten people live in cities of 20,000 or more population. According to the *Population Bulletin* of September,
1960, published by the Population Reference Bureau, Inc.,
almost half of the world's population will live in cities of this
size by 2000 (and by 2050, nine people out of every ten) for
there is every likelihood that the present trend will continue.
According to preliminary calculations based on the 1960
census, the New York metropolitan conurbation has a population of over 14.5 million; that is more than the population of
Australia and New Zealand combined.

In comparison with this inflated giant, Calcutta has a
relatively small population of only 5.7 million. But, according
to the *Bulletin,* estimates based on present trends give Calcutta a population of 35 to 66 million by 2000, in an area of
the size of Rhode Island! The value of these projections lies
less, let us hope, in their realistic possibilities than in the fact
that they point out the great dangers of this development if
it continues unchecked. It is most likely that a growth of

these dimensions will be self-defeating and that the difficulty of food supply, housing, and sanitation would work against this fantastic multiplication.

But where and how can the population increase be absorbed? Can the cities of tomorrow remain the centers of attraction and culture, or will they become mere refuse dumps for human beings? Can we expect that the chaotic and inefficient cities of the West, lagging far behind this tempestuous development, will be able to cope with this situation? Reforms of a minor character and even large-scale improvements are not enough to solve these problems. Only the boldest actions on a global scale and a radical break with the past may turn the tide and hold out a promise of success.

I do not intend to bore readers with elaborate statistics. But certain facts should be mentioned. They are irrefutable evidence of the high price we have to pay now and even more so in the future, if our cities continue to develop on the same lines as up to the present. Today more than 20 per cent of the world population, that is, more than 500 million, live in urban communities of 20,000 or more, and over three-fifths of them (13 per cent of the world population) live in cities of 100,000 or more inhabitants.

The *Report on the World Social Situation,* published by the United Nations in 1957, discussed, among other matters, present and future trends of urbanization in relation to population growth in underdeveloped areas:

A major factor in the present and the anticipated future acceleration is the sudden spurt of urban growth in economically underdeveloped countries. Between 1900 and 1950, the population living in cities of 100,000 or more in Asia mounted from an estimated 19.4 million to 105.6 million (a gain of 444 per cent), and in Africa from 1.4 million to 10.2 million (a gain of 629 per cent).

. . . the large-city population of Asia and Africa has increased much more rapidly during the twentieth century than it did during the nineteenth century while in Europe and America, urban growth reached its peak in the latter part of the nineteenth century and slowed down thereafter. These shifting rates of growth have meant that Asia, which contained nearly two-thirds of the world's population in large cities in 1800, had less than a fourth by 1900; but then the trend started to reverse, and by 1950 Asia had one-third of the world's large-city population. . . . In the majority of the less developed countries, the rural population has continued to grow along with the urban population, although at a slower pace, but in many of the developed countries the absolute size of the rural population has remained constant or even declined in recent decades, so that the national population increase has been absorbed by the already heavy urban population. [And as regards] the overflow of rural distress into urban districts [the Report remarks:] The rapidly growing cities of the less developed regions of the world generally have several districts or zones which are imperfectly integrated: (1) A modern commercial, administrative, and upper-class residential centre; (2) An "old city" of narrow streets and densely occupied buildings; (3) A zone of huts or shacks, within or without the city limits proper, lacking most urban features except density of settlement and urban types of employment among the residents. This pattern has many variations. In some cases, particularly in Asia and North Africa, the modern city is completely separate from the old, and the latter has retained its traditional artisan industries, commercial activities (e.g. bazaars) and social organization, often being divided into sharply defined quarters along ethnic or religious lines. A few of the old cities (e.g. Damascus) have grown to considerable size with only a minor admixture of modern elements. In other cases, particularly in Latin America, the modern city and the old are intermingled, with the recent expansion of the former sometimes almost obliterating the latter, or reducing it to a zone of deteriorating tenement houses. In most of Africa south of the Sahara, and in various industrial, mining, and oil-producing centres in other regions, the old city has never existed. The zone of huts or shacks is usually on the periphery of the city. In some cases it is made up of coherent villages maintaining traditional values and social controls similar to those of the rural villages; more frequently however, this zone consists largely of amorphous mushrooming shantytowns, lacking any formal administration or any apparent informal social organization. Such shantytowns may be outside the administrative boundary of the city, so that no authority is responsible for providing urban services and enforcing housing regulations. . . . The pattern of urban growth is also complicated by the location of factories, usually around the periphery of the cities; their workers may come from neighbouring shantytowns or from more substantial workers' housing built by the employers or the state.

In the Western countries, already heavily urbanized, where urbanization has spread over larger regions than in the underdeveloped areas, the progressing growth of the urban population seems to have been accepted as an act of providence. The same fatalism influences our attitude toward the effects this increase in size and numbers will have upon the social problems concomitant with this development. If we cannot be prophets of the future, we should be at least prophets in reverse and learn from the present and the past what we should avoid at all costs.

We should admit that social pressures and tensions will intensify, that juvenile delinquency and adult criminality will become worse and more widespread, that traffic, air pollution, slums, and substandard houses will put an immense burden on the financial capacity of the metropolitan conglomeration, and that all the innumerable public services will be entirely inadequate. All this will be unavoidable, if urbanization and urban growth continue unchecked, and if we believe that a mere extension of some social and economic institutions is sufficient to cope with the dangerous problems that the glorification of quantity and bigness piles up before our eyes. Then it will be too late to pay even a very exorbitant price to remedy a situation that has already gone beyond redress.

This is not a Cassandra cry evoked by present failures. It is a sober estimate based on serious studies by professional people. What do they see ahead for a megalopolis such as New York? As a critic of one of these studies put it: "The same thing we have today. Only more of it. Much more." More proof that this fatalistic attitude is rather common could easily be adduced.

It is a disquieting fact that the numerous study groups that have sprung up during the last years are more concerned with methods and institutional devices, hectically trying to preserve the essence of the old structure, however inadequate this may be, than with searching for new ideas and new solutions and then adapting methods and institutions as framework to the new structure. These groups believe that a treatment of the symptoms will produce results. They fail to see that only a determined offensive against the causes can hold out any hope of decisive and lasting success.

There is, however, a ray of hope, although in comparison with other countries the number of farsighted people in the United States who are aware of the disastrous consequences of this half-hearted laissez-faire policy is still small. The warnings of this minority that only large regional schemes and far-reaching and systematic decentralization of the urban conglomerations can lead us out of the impasse are still drowned by the pontificating of the apostles of "free enterprise" and of the "it is after all not as bad as that" attitude.

But we may hope that the voices of reason and the hard facts of life will gradually arouse public opinion and alert it to the great problems created by the rapid increase of population and the insane belief in the dogma that it is the mission of a city to grow without restraint.

In this connection it is impossible, and not even desirable, to deal with all the innumerable problems which impinge on urban existence. Let us select only two of the more obvious aspects, to which the man in the street has perhaps given some thought because he experiences their influence directly in daily life. There is the problem of leisure and the impact of technology. I cannot pay more than a cursory attention to these topical questions. But I would refer readers to the considerable literature on these subjects, where they will find quite a few excellent treatises based on solid research and full of intuitive insights.

Here it may be sufficient to stress just a few implications which affect the life of the masses. Today, everybody wants to gain time, but hardly anybody knows what to do with it, when he has gained it. The result is a peculiar sort of private unemployment and a flight into a "do-it-yourself" pottering about. The mass media of communication are finding an ever-increasing public that listens willy-nilly to programs attuned to the low level of mass consumption.

In a despiritualized world leisure has become a synonym for boredom; something almost sinister; something that is desirable and yet, at the same time, disquieting. How many people are longing to go back to work after a free weekend because they do not know how to kill their time? I doubt that this same attitude would exist in an inspiring environment, an environment our cities cannot offer.

Hence, we see the almost unlimited gullibility of the masses and the standardized manner in which they make use of their daily leisure. They watch the same films; they listen to the same radio programs; they read the same magazines filled with mediocre articles on "what the public wants." In other words, their leisure is prefabricated for them, and psychological mass manipulation has a field day. Vacations are organized with alluring promises of "living in a grand style."

Let there be no mistake: this is an international problem, an international symptom of all technological societies, independent of political, social, and economic systems. This is our present situation. But what about the future when these trends, to all appearances, will be even more outspoken? I believe that there is some hope of improvement, when and if our physical and cultural environment becomes more diversified, more exciting, offering more outlets for individual creativity.

In their excellent document, *Industrialism and Industrial Man*, Professors Kerr of the University of California, Dunlop of Harvard University, Harbison of Princeton University, and Myers of the Massachusetts Institute of Technology say:

The great new freedom may come in the leisure of individuals. Higher standards of living, more leisure, more education make this not only possible but almost inevitable. This will be the happy hunting ground for the independent spirit. Along with the bureaucratic conservatism of economic and political life may well go a New Bohemianism in the other aspects of life and partly as a reaction to the confining nature of the productive side of society. There may well come a new search for individuality and a new meaning of liberty. The economic system may be highly ordered and the political system barren ideologically; but the social and recreational and cultural aspects of life diverse and changing.

Let us hope that these expectations will prove to be true. But let us also add that they can materialize only after a revolution of our physical and cultural environment.

Technology and leisure are intimately interrelated. The more automation progresses and the more thinking is done for us by computers, the more time is set free for leisure. It is a vicious circle which can only be broken by intense efforts and great changes in our mentality and in our ways of living.

Industry will produce the same and even a greater quantity of goods with fewer workers in fewer working hours, and agriculture will become more and more a branch of chemistry and automative industrial production, driving ever increasing numbers of people from the country to the cities. At the same time the progress of automation will increasingly dissociate the worker from his work.

This poses a new problem, for, as Freud has explained in *Das Unbehagen in der Kultur (Civilization and Its Discontent)*, work is an eminently creative factor of fulfillment and self-expression for the individual. Thus, the gap between the functional and the personal life of the masses widens, without any compensation, as far as can be seen at the moment, for this unsettling transformation.

Oddly enough, it seems that for the time being the increased leisure is used for working. Several surveys in this and other countries have established the fact that a considerable number of workers have second full-time or part-time jobs. Caught in this vicious circle of work-leisure-wages, time which could have been developed for intellectual improvement and enjoyment of valuable cultural activities is helplessly bartered for the doubtful and leveling-down gifts of mass media running amok.

Can we expect these men to take an active interest in their community without ever-present and powerful incen-

tives to break through the barriers of their narrowly circum-
scribed existence? Can those sorely needed incentives be
provided in our big cities, where the majority of these workers live? To put the question is to give the answer.

City planners and architects do not possess a magic
wand with which to change our environment over night, nor
are they the sole agents of this formidable task. But they
should be at least in the forefront of those who are responsible for environmental transformations. I believe that they
are in many respects well equipped to make constructive
contributions to the solution of these problems.

The revolution in architecture and in other arts has been
greater than in many other fields. It has advanced far beyond
conventional pragmatism, and has opened new vistas which
are still closed in the social, economic, and political spheres.
And let us repeat, although I am aware of the possible mis-
givings of some of my readers, that nothing can be changed
in the inner life of an individual without changing simultaneously his physical and cultural environment, and that this
can only be done by a far-reaching and fundamental reshaping of all its aspects, not by isolated and minor reforms of a
few sectors only.

But can it be done in present conditions? There can be
no doubt that we are capable of doing it. Our scientific and
technical achievements in the exploration of space are an
encouraging proof. The question is rather: do we want to do
it? This is the crux of the matter. And here grave doubts
exist. The retarding forces of the Establishment, private and
public, as represented by Big Business and the Government,
are more interested in preserving the *status quo* than in bold
actions that by their very nature are never free of a certain
risk.

It will be a hard fight to rip up the net which the superconscious protagonists of the *status quo* have thrown over the mind of the masses, and to undermine their dominating position as the self-appointed guardians of a so-called stability and a pseudo commonsense. But it can be done, if this attack is carried forward with determination, sincerity, intelligence, and insight.

The first step is to investigate the potentialities of our situation. The second step is to formulate these potentialities, their aims and direction, in a clear program that can be understood by the man in the street, and to show him in an intelligible and concrete form what he can expect. The last part of this work will, I hope, give some indication of how this can be made a sensible proposition and how it can be presented in a simple and demonstrative form.

An aggravating factor is that environment and city planning are the most backward sectors of public enterprise, hampered partly by material difficulties and its great complexity, but even more so by the vested interests of profit-seeking developers, and the lack of vision and audacity of the "coordinators" who are responsible for these matters. Their masterly incompetence is surpassed only by their self-perpetuating and unshakable conviction that they cannot do more than they are doing and that theirs is the right and only way in which to deal with the pressing problems of our situation.

I am often haunted by a feeling that the time is not far off when someone will be able to change my thoughts with a machine, and deprive me of my own capacity to think. I am afraid that in the field of city planning some clever and powerful people are already busily trying to manipulate my thinking, and that of many others, without our being aware of it, toward maintaining the *status quo* and being content with what they hope to convince us is "what the public wants," but what in reality is what they want to impose on the public.

There are, of course, many conscientious and serious municipal officials who have no share in this selling of "packaged" houses in "packaged" communities. But this trend does exist, and the danger of these tendencies for city planning in general should not be underestimated. In his *The Hidden Persuaders*, Vance Packard quotes the description of a new "community," Miramar, Florida, published by *Time:*

To make Miramar as homey and congenial as possible, the builders have established what might be called "regimented recreation." As soon as a family moves in, the lady of the house will get an invitation to join any number of activities ranging from bridge games to library teas. Her husband will be introduced, by Miramar, to local groups interested in anything from fish breeding to water skiing.

Here lies the danger of direct and indirect mass manipulation under the cover of pleasant and easy social cooperation. Let us hope that more and more people will see through these attempts at a cheap and seemingly innocent diversion from independent and progressive thinking.

So far, city planning has not even remotely used the great possibility which science and technology offers. It is really not enough to build marvelous highways, to drive tunnels under rivers, to spread veritable underground cities below the visible urban agglomerations, and to erect buildings with an air-conditioned artificial atmosphere, with artificial light in large sections. We know that we can do all this but we do not know, or we refuse to know, that it has nothing to do with a full and creative use of science and technology that would fundamentally change the face of our environment.

On the contrary, all these efforts preserve the *status quo*. They do not add one single new and basic idea to city planning from which a fresh start could be made. Behind all this is the dislike of the unlike, the fear of the unknown. Hence the schizophrenic attitude of many business people whose offices and plants cannot be modern and rational enough but whose private homes are showpieces of *n*th-rate period pieces and romantic sentimentalism or of *Kitsch* and family monstrosities

No—science and technology are not yet part and parcel of our civilization; that is, they are still the admired, misused, and misunderstood fetishes with which the witch-doctors, the Scientists, conjure up the spirits of progress and happiness that have the fatal habit of dissolving into air as soon as they threaten to recast the raw materials of our existence and to reshape our environment in its innumerable aspects. They are still outsiders, whose impact is felt but dreaded except when they help to make what is, not what could be, more convenient and possibly cheaper.

A trend away from the integration of science and technology, away from conformity and superficiality, can be initiated only if the imaginative and creative faculties of the individual are released and given full scope for self-expression. As Lord Adrian warned at the third World Congress of Psychiatry at Montreal in 1961:

If science is to survive, it must be creative in a wider sphere than that of the material basis of living organisms or living behaviour. We are badly in need of the new discoveries and the new ideas which will help us to understand how the behaviour of the individual organism can be regulated so that the community of individuals will survive, how, in fact, human societies can live contentedly with one another. Unless social science can be as creative as natural science our new tools are not likely to be much use to us.

Unfortunately, these words are only too true. The sociologists, whose task it should be to enlighten and assist the city planners, fail to supply any really valuable guidance. Their ideas, methods, and tools are still primitive, although they flatter themselves to be social "scientists." But so far their efforts have resulted only in a pseudo science. This is not their fault. The foundations on which their work could firmly rest are still too shaky, and what they want to achieve is so ambitious that no single science, least of all our present sociology, can hope to disentangle the plexus of the innumerable traits that make up the human character and determine human actions.

The enthusiastic social researchers who investigate a new or old community try to find out what people want, what their motives and ambitions are—why they settled, for instance, in one of the ready-made standardized communities —and how they live. Their usual method is to send out questionnaires, to interrogate hundreds of people, and to check and recheck the results before formulating general observations and producing statistics and diagrams.

It may be permissible to suggest with the greatest humility that there are certain problems that they cannot solve by these methods, not even with the most diligent preparation and work. Do people really know what they want, what their motives are, what other possibilities exist? And can we be quite sure that the researchers ask the right, the really relevant questions, and that they possess the rare gift of insight and understanding that often are the result of brilliant artistic shortcuts?

But let us not blame the researchers. The instruments that they have at their disposal are still inefficient and may lead them astray. Tolstoy, aware of the influence of the unpredictable vagaries of human nature, of the irrational impulses that motivate human decisions, made this plain when he spoke in *War and Peace,* to mention only one of his numerous statements on this problem, of the "illogical phenomena . . . of which we see the causation but darkly, and which only seem the more illogical the more earnestly we strive to account for them"; or when he says of Kutuzow that this old man used "quite meaningless words that happened to enter his head," for he had "by experience of life reached the conclusion that thoughts, and words serving their expression, are not what move people."

It would not be surprising if these words were dismissed by professional sociologists as pleasant musings of an idealistic writer who did not have to deal with the "hard facts of life." I am afraid sociologists and like-minded people who discard these insights are not on firm ground. So far poets and writers and nonprofessional publicists have possibly made greater contributions to our understanding of human nature than all professionals of all countries combined.

This statement, will, I am sure, draw upon me the wrath and the ridicule of these numerous and dedicated experts, but since it is always encouraging to be in good company, I would remind them that the number of people who are skeptical of their work is growing and that among these skeptics are many more men of the eminence of Lord Adrian.

It is not suggested that the social researchers should give up their efforts, but merely that they should try to perfect themselves before trying to understand others, and that city planners and other persons who may wish to use their work should be very careful and not rely blindly on the results presented to them. The fault of sociological research lies in the fact that it approaches the human problem from without, not from within, the human personality, and that its methods are derived from and adapted to this external approach.

To conclude this chapter with a note of optimism: in a field that may seem to be far removed from city planning, in the sphere of the Cold War, a world-wide revulsion against this travesty of a battle of ideas is spreading. The weapons of the Cold War are deceptive propaganda, distortion, omissions, outright lies, and in general a denial of any positive qualities to the adversary, with a corresponding self-righteous glorification of the virtues of one's own country.

The rebellion against this sterile and one-sided "anti-attitude" is gaining momentum. People begin to see through the fog of propaganda, and the nimbus of politicians and statesmen is losing its charismatic appeal. One is tempted to paraphrase a famous slogan and to shout at these "leaders": figureheads of the world, unite. You have nothing to lose but a war; but living under the pleasant protection of a mutual deterrent, we may be hopeful that this will not happen.

There is, however, another danger that is more real and that has already produced unfortunate and far-reaching results. Can anyone really believe that the mentality of the Cold War, now going on for fifteen years, will disappear overnight, if the unforeseen should happen and real peace in our time break out? Is it possible to expect that the fall-out of this Cold War propaganda will leave no traces behind?

Basically this attitude is a revival of the old hostility that existed between the in-group and the out-group of primitive peoples that bred overestimation of one's own civilization and contempt of and aggressiveness toward other civilizations. It produced a strange combination of uncertainty and inferiority with a bragging and overbearing self-approbation. Today we are face to face with a new version of this predicament that has plagued mankind for thousands of years. The appealing but disturbing notion of "peaceful coexistence," which in any case is, apart from its political implications, better than universal annihilation, has revived the antagonism between the in-group and the out-group on a global scale.

This primitive anachronism, which derives not only its main strength but its final cause from being "against" and not "for" something, has so permeated men's minds that it affects all our thoughts and actions. City planning is no exception. Every city official, every city planner, wants to grab as much land, as much tax money, as many inhabitants, as many outlying districts as possible for his own city. The hunt for these coveted prizes, this civic buccaneering and uneasy coexistence between cities has hardly anything in common with constructive and peaceful competition.

It is still too early to predict with any degree of certainty how lasting or intense the impact of this confrontation will be on the minds of men, but there seems to develop a certain restiveness, a certain opposition among the masses against this primeval and dangerous relic of what has been called the *Urdummheit*, Primal Stupidity. This is a hopeful sign. The masses want deeds, not words and promises. The opposition against being conditioned is growing, especially among the younger generations of the world.

As city planning is an eminently collective public activity, it may be affected by the spread of a rediscovered skepticism. Far-fetched? I do not think so. Life is an indissoluble whole, and cities are one of the most intricate creations of mankind, where all the innumerable threads of our existence are deeply woven into the fabric of being. As I said before, city planning has been and still is full of antiquated and empty slogans, and little, if anything, has been done to discard them and to open a new vision in which people can enthusiastically believe. Skepticism and doubt are the harbingers of change. This is our hope, and since both are beginning to penetrate ever widening circles of the peoples of the world, we might expect that our cities and the man-made and natural environment will benefit from this awakening.

WHY DO PEOPLE
LIVE IN CITIES?

Are those reasons still valid which for thousands of years have driven people to the cities, creating, in our own time, sprawling conurbations and vast urbanized landscapes? Urban ways of living, or at least their surrogates, and an unfulfilled longing for the amenities and distractions of city life have engulfed more people than are actually living in cities. About half of the world's population is engaged in agricultural pursuits, but a considerable number of these countrymen have adopted the habits and ideas of city-dwellers, or are potential urbanites.

This development is not merely the result of the spread of surface values. It is rather a deep infiltration of ideas and material forces that transforms the whole outlook on life and draws the thoughts and work of the peasants into the vortex of revolutionary changes originating in the cities. From the cities, growing more and more amorphous economically and socially, there have been spreading forces that exert an ever-increasing impact on the rural areas, disintegrating old ways of living and creating a new attitude toward life. These forces are moving toward the same goal, toward an integration of all parts of large regions. This development will grow in intensity and lead to unity in diversity encompassing whole countries.

The fact that we still think in terms of city and country, and try to superimpose a new social pattern of which we have but a very hazy idea on the existing urban structure proves our incapability of breaking away from outworn notions. The "City" concept is an anachronism, and even far-reaching reforms cannot prevent its decay and final disappearance. It is a concept that dates back to the time of the first city builders. It has lasted 5,000 years. It took root because men were yearning for security and proximity and because they developed more differentiated habits and needs.

The Urban Revolution was one of the greatest events in the history of mankind, comparable only to the great leap forward that the mind of man experienced in the fifth century B.C., and perhaps to the Scientific Revolution that hit its full stride some 250 years ago. The first cities were built in opposition to the countryside. They were the result of a new feeling of space. They were cut out from the surrounding natural environment and entirely man-made. They were a flight from insecurity and isolation and from the spiritual dangers of Nature, from her demons and her unforeseeable powers. They opened the floodgates of the creative mind of man to the adventures of art and philosophy, of civic life and technical progress, till today the whole human existence has been overwhelmed by the superficiality of an "as if" civilization, and by the acceptance of half-truths as final revelations.

When we ask why people live in cities, we should add a secondary question: what needs can be provided for only in cities and what needs elsewhere?

Principles of Integration and Types of Institution

There is no real difference between sociology and anthropology. Being what we are, we call what concerns ourselves sociology and what concerns primitive man anthropology. Whether this is just a difference in terminology or something more significant, the scientific attitude of an eminent anthropologist will certainly be a useful guide through our argument. I have made, therefore, ample use of the principles that Professor Malinowski has developed in *A Scientific Theory of Culture*. He groups universal institutional types under seven headings, in each case juxtaposing the principles of integration and the types of institution.

The first group concerns reproduction, that is, bonds of blood defined by legal contract of marriage:

The institutional type which answers this principle is the family, as the domestic group of parents and children; courtship organization; the legal definition and organization of marriage as a contract binding two individuals and relating two groups; the extended domestic group and its legal, economic, and religious organization.

None of these institutions is restricted to urban areas. They are common to all types of settlement. The only minor difference, though this too is disappearing in almost all parts of the world, is that the "extended domestic group" is still somewhat more evident in the country than in the cities.

The second group comprises territorial principles of integration and their corresponding institutions. Community of interest due to propinquity, continuity, and possibly to cooperation "exist in neighbourhood groups of all types; such as the village, the cluster of hamlets or homesteads, the town, the city, the district, the province, the tribe"—or, if this is more acceptable, the nation. One might be inclined to suggest that community of interest has a more personal character in small neighborhood groups, but this is counterbalanced by the greater frictions that are inevitably connected with the more permanent companionship, and the reduced self-discipline in smaller units, bringing out aggressive character traits that are more likely to be kept back in more impersonal surroundings.

The third group refers to psychological principles of integration as expressed by "distinction due to sex, age, and bodily stigmata or symptoms," and their corresponding institutions, such as

organizations based on psychological or anatomical sex distinctions, or due to sexual division of functions and activities; age-groups or age-grades insofar as they are organized; and institutions for the sick, the insane, the congenitally defective.

All these types of institutions can be found in every community, possibly with somewhat better services for the infirm in urban districts—at the present. This, however, is only a temporary drawback and would disappear with the development of regional integration.

The fourth group of principles of integration consists of voluntary associations, and the types of institutions are "clubs, mutual aid and benefit societies, lodges, voluntary associations for recreation, uplift, or the realization of a common purpose." All these institutions are based on voluntary decisions. They need no help, or, if at all, only a slight encouragement and assistance from official bodies. They are in existence everywhere and completely independent of the size or place of neighborhood groups.

The fifth group concerns occupational and professional organizations "of human beings by their specialized activities for the purpose of common interests and a fuller achievement of the special abilities." The institutional types which belong to these principles are:

the innumerable workshops, guilds, and undertakings, economic interest groups, and associations of professional workers in medicine, in law, in teaching, and in ministering to religious needs. Also specific units for the organized exercise of teaching (schools, colleges, universities); for research (laboratories, academies, institutes); for administration of justice (legislative bodies, courts, police force); for defense and aggression (army, navy, air force); for religion (parish, sects, churches).

The general types mentioned first are spread in all parts of the world over the whole country, differentiated only in so far as they are dependent on natural resources or on comprehensive organizations, with branches in many, though not in all, places and with head offices mostly, though not always, in big cities. The specific units extend likewise over the whole country graded in importance according to their local, regional and national functions.

Essentially, hardly any of the general or of the specific

types must be located in one particular place. They are more or less "foot-loose," quite apart from the fact that a great number are, in any case, distributed over the whole area of the country. Not even the central administration and the central assembly need be in a big city.

As the sixth group we have integration by rank and status, a principle that is rapidly losing in importance. Its institutional types are:

Estates and orders of nobility, clergy, burghers, peasants, serfs, slaves, the caste system, and stratification by ethnic, that is, either racial or cultural distinctions at primitive and developed levels.

It is difficult to advance any reasons for the continuance of these institutions and therefore for their location in any particular place. As far as these groupings distinguish between peasants and burghers they are identical with occupational types.

Finally, the seventh group. Malinowski calls this principle of integration comprehensive. It refers to integration by community of culture or by political power, and its types of integration are:

The tribe as the cultural unit corresponding to nationality at more highly developed levels. The cultural sub-group in the regional sense or in the sense of small enclaves (alien minorities, the ghetto, the gypsies). The political unit which may comprise part of a tribe-nation and tribe-state as a political organization is fundamental.

These institutions, which are, of course, essential, are entirely independent of geographical location. Culture comprises the whole complex of activities within the whole territory of a people. The assumption that there can be something like an urban and rural culture is erroneous. And as regards "cultural" institutions it is extremely doubtful whether the noisy and commercialized entertainment industry has anything to do with culture even in its widest sense.

Museums and libraries and similar institutions can be made "mobile"; their objects of art and books should not be fixed in one place. In any case, there is no cogent reason to restrict them to the big cities. As to the political aspects, cultural integration cannot accept any tutelage from political quarters, whether they are instruments of the "tribe-nation" or the "tribe-state."

Integration means completeness and the creative combination of constituent parts. It is not a mere putting together of different functions, but the mutual penetration of all functions which pertain to a particular type of integration into one indivisible whole. And above all, genuine integration cannot be achieved in space only, or in time only. It is rather the result of functions working in time and space as one inseparable whole.

If we accept the principles of integration enumerated by Malinowski, and if we agree with his types of institutions, it is obvious that principles as well as types are not restricted to a particular space or to a particular time, but are operative everywhere and at any time, with a few minor exceptions that do not alter the essence of our conclusions.

Are there any institutions which can operate only in cities, or, to put it more generally, in localities the characteristics of which are (a) a considerable number of people and (b) a conglomeration of these people within a relatively narrow space? The reply can only be: there are none. We shall deal with this problem later and in more detail.

What is it that attracts people to cities? In present conditions it is, broadly speaking, work, wages, social contacts, and entertainment. No real cure is possible, however, for the isolation and narrowness of the masses in rural areas, towns, and cities before fundamental changes in our social concepts and institutions have grown so strong that they revolutionize the physical environment and wipe out the antagonism between city and country.

It is not true that life in cities is less isolated than in the country. It is merely another sort of isolation. In the cities this isolation, this human desert, is superficially hidden by the agitation and variety on the surface, and in the country by the rhythm of nature, imposing a rigid equality of life in time and space upon the members of a rural community.

It is an illusion, and a very dangerous one at that, to think of our cities as something that cannot be changed fundamentally, as something that can only be transformed on the surface and reformed in detail. We fail to understand that cities are themselves mere details, that regions and countries, continents and the world are the realistic units of man's living space. The present structure of our cities has developed during the lifetime of the last five to six generations. The forces that before this time have made cities and have given them their physical shape have died away.

Today, cities are vehicles for certain functions, working through a number of institutions that are lifeless organizations catering to economic needs, but not life-centered organisms grown out of and taking care of social aspirations and values. Most of our institutions are like the dry bed of a river that has changed its course or has completely disappeared. The belief in the indispensability of proximity has been lingering on from medieval times, when life proceeded at a more leisurely pace, more through personal contacts and on a pedestrian scale.

Today all this has changed: time is money and life has become impersonal and hectic. The pedestrian scale has been superseded by the scale of the motor car, the telephone, and the mail. The spirit of the guilds with their personal relationship has given way to the rationalism of large-scale organizations. The factories, which produce the goods that are administered in the city offices, are far away. The money accumulated in and redistributed from the cities runs through the finest channels to all parts of the country.

A small number of enterprises have understood this development and have moved away from the crowded urban centers, without any disadvantage to the conduct of their affairs. This tendency is slowly growing, but it is still unsystematic, and dependent on individual decisions that may produce unfavorable effects in the new places to which the business has been transferred because an over-all guidance is lacking. Without planning on a large scale no sound balance between individual communities can be expected, and no social integration can result.

The motive power behind these moves is purely economic. Even if the State tries to regulate the redistribution of industry and commercial offices, it does so only in a preventive way, marking out districts and towns to which factories or offices should not be moved. In any case social considerations cannot play any role, for social integration cannot be created to order.

Cultural Imperatives

In addition to the seven principles of integration and the corresponding types of institutions, Malinowski offers, although in a somewhat different context, another criterion, by reducing the problem to four cultural imperatives and to four responses to these imperatives. They confirm the same principle, namely, that a new pattern of living within a revolutionized environment does not impose any restrictions in time or space on this interplay of challenge and response. In other words, city life in the old sense is not a prerequisite of creative responses to what Malinowski calls the instrumental imperatives of culture.

The first is: "the cultural apparatus of implements and consumers' goods must be produced, used, maintained, and replaced by new production." The response is: economics. It may be objected that certain industries must be in cities and that others are fixed on the natural resources they process. I do not wish to anticipate the suggestions for a redistribution of population and for regional and national integration, but this much may be said here. The old concept of a city as a sort of cauldron where all the main economic activities are heated up to boiling point until they overflow into the country cannot serve as a yardstick.

We must visualize the situation in about three generations' time. Then a more equal distribution of population and industry will have taken place. Cities, towns, and villages will be integrated communities. They will vary in size and numbers of inhabitants but not so much in character. The whole region will be one good dwelling, and cities in the old sense as dominating centers drawing people, industries, offices, and cultural activities away from smaller towns and rural places will have disappeared.

Life and work in all communities of a region will proceed on an equal level. As in numerous communicating pipes, the level of quality in all spheres of life will be the same, and the fact that a few places have more inhabitants will not be a qualification for greater attraction and far less for a domineering preponderance.

The presence of industries will not determine the cultural character of a community. They will not be like a tumor producing a morbid growth in the social body of the community. Hitherto all towns and rural places have suffered from the aggressive absorption of the big cities in their region. They were like forgotten and neglected relatives, whose presence is tolerated but who must be kept in their place. And just as these poor relations often develop a defense mechanism, overplaying their own importance and retreating into a narrow self-admiration, so the small towns and rural communities resort to a cheap parochialism that in its deeper meaning is the overcompensation of a collective inferiority complex caused by the overbearing and condescending attitude of the big cities.

The mobility of industry has increased ever since the introduction of electricity as power supply; it is certain that this development will gain in momentum as soon as atomic energy can be made more available. It goes beyond the scope of this book to discuss the location of industry. I have done this in detail elsewhere.* A relatively small number of industries are not mobile, such as those based on coal, or ports, and, of course, on the cultivation of the soil. But this need not lead to overgrown conglomerations or to conurbations. Many ancillary industries that are today located near the basic industries can be moved to other places without any disadvantages to the cost and efficiency of production.

The second imperative concerns human behavior. "As regards its technical, customary, legal, or moral prescription it must be codified, regulated in action and sanction." The

---

* *Creative Demobilization,* 1943.

response is: social control. After all that has been explained on the foregoing pages there is no need to elaborate this point. Social control can be exercised everywhere, although it must never become an instrument of coercion that would curtail the spontaneity and independent decisions of the people.

The third imperative: "The Human Material by which every institution is maintained must be renewed, formed, drilled, and provided with full knowledge of tribal tradition" —or rather, I would add, provided with a high responsibility toward the environment, with a keen sense of the possibilities that point the way to the future and with a stimulating sensibility to values. The response is: education, but an education that aims at developing full man, that strives to remove the blinkers of a predominantly professional training, and that is universal for all ages. It would include provisions for recreation and leisure—two distinctly different tasks—and educational institutions spread out over the whole country. Institutes for higher education can be located in any place where certain prerequisites are fulfilled. They do not depend on the number of people living in a locality but rather on the most suitable environment. There is no reason that they should be in urban surroundings.

Finally the fourth imperative: "Authority within each institution must be defined, equipped with powers, and endowed with means of forceful execution of the orders." The response is: political organization. I have mentioned this last point because I wanted to give a complete picture of Malinowski's four imperatives. I believe, however, that this last one needs a certain qualification. It sounds somewhat totalitarian, though I am convinced that its author would have strongly deprecated any such intention.

I would offer the following criticism: political power is not the same as political organization, although they may often be overlapping. The first is something working from above and the second something that may and indeed should grow from the bottom. The first is a response whose disappearance is devoutly to be desired. It belongs to the realm of the uncreative State, while the second might become creative, if it is kept free from the corrupting influence of a dominant minority. That political organization is a ubiquitous response is obvious.

The double test of the reaction between principles of integration and types of institution, on the one hand, and between imperatives and responses on the other applied to the question, "Why do people live in cities?" should prove that purely practical reasons can hardly offer a satisfactory explanation. It is more likely that emotional motives play a more decisive role and that these urges are turned afterwards into rationalized considerations. In present conditions it is, of course, easier to find work and better services and to satisfy the gregarious instinct in cities than in small communities or rural districts, but this is exclusively the result of the unquestioning acceptance of trends that have developed in the past and belong to the past.

EXTERNAL AND
INTERNAL REFORMS

That this concentration of population and industry in urban areas leads to disaster has been recognized by a few well-meaning and farsighted persons. Their aim was to relieve the pressure by external and internal reforms. The first results in the establishment of new towns within the sphere of influence of big cities, and the second in "the discovery of the third dimension."

The first is a remedy somewhat in the nature of artificial insemination, producing a new child with all the disadvantages of a half-known parentage and without the stimulating excitement that this adventure into the unknown could evoke. The result is the Garden City, now rechristened the New Town Movement.

The second is a surgical operation, cutting out unhealthy parts of the urban body and grafting on new structures. This is a sort of plastic surgery that results in the pulling down of slum quarters and the erection of high buildings surrounded by open spaces.

The Garden City idea is a pleasant romanticism of the late Victorians. It is, in addition to artificial insemination, a homeopathic treatment by which, according to the exact definition of this theory, the "malady is cured by frequent minute doses of a drug which normally produces symptoms like those of the malady itself." This is truer than it may appear at the first glance.

The Garden City is the embodiment of the eternal small-town ideal. It suffers from the same stuffiness, the same dependence on the big cities, and the same lack of a social program. One of its leading principles was "how to restore the people to the land." That sounds very progressive, and it certainly was at the time when Ebenezer Howard, the protagonist of this idea, published his book, *To-morrow,* in 1898.

A Garden City, and for that matter any New Town, is born with two inherent ailments. If it is a more or less self-contained town with a sufficient diversity of industry, so that at least a considerable portion of the local population can work there, it will inevitably develop the provincial narrowness and frustration that are the unavoidable by-products of small-town life as long as physical decentralization is not accompanied by cultural and social decentralization.

If a sufficient number of industries cannot be attracted, it will become one of the numerous dormitory towns, entirely dependent on the city for which it was expected to act as a draining-off reservoir. The journey to work that most of the inhabitants have to make every day renders the idea of restoring the people to the land rather illusory, while the housewives become world-forgetting and by-the-world-forgotten domestic machines.

The Garden City cannot offer a solution for evils that lie at the root of the social and economic problems. It was conceived at a time when the belief in a static society was still unshaken and the idea of a new dynamic era had not yet dawned even upon the most enlightened spirits. Today, the Garden City is still the gospel of many reformers who believe in the efficiency of half-measures within the existing order. They fail to see that even the best intentions are doomed to failure if they cannot produce anything but isolated actions. They are moving within a vicious circle of complacency and illusion.

The Garden City is the typical product of the neurosis that is so characteristic of the lower middle class; wedged in between the upper strata of society and the workers, it suffers from a social claustrophobia. Clandestinely it admires the upper classes, and especially the hereditary and moneyed aristocracy, while it is afraid of the lower groups and terrified that it may be proletarianized.

Audacity has never been a conspicuous character trait

of the lower middle class. Its life was, and still is, an *ad hoc* existence. Security, conformity, and respectability are its main ambitions. To live for the future, to be stimulated by evolution in action, and to be the instigators of revolutionary ideas has never been its mission as a class.

The main objection to the concept of Garden Cities is, however, the unfortunate obstinacy of its promoters, who try to uphold an ideal which belongs to the past. In its time it was the perfect expression of benevolent and sincere intentions. But these intentions were determined by the ideas and possibilities of the period. They are the product of fractional thinking and of an evasion of the real issues.

The much advertised New Towns of England are the slightly revised edition of the original Garden City. They are perhaps better architecturally, though the results are so far discouraging. A few more social services may be available, but fundamentally they will remain small towns with small-town folk. The regional schemes of which they are to be a part are far from being cultural and economic entities: they are not even the starting point of a new pattern of living, and they are not designed as part and parcel of a national plan within which the national and provincial metropolises and the cities will lose their absorbing preponderance in all cultural, social, and economic activities.

In short, the New Towns will not be equal partners in a centerless dispersion of these activities, but will remain dependent on the old centers. At best they will be a useful demonstration of the final futility of the Garden City idea, and at worst frustrated hybrids with the disadvantage of city and country but without the positive attractions of either. They are an end, not a beginning. They are not communities but artificially created units of living within the old pattern of the social and economic environment.

The internal operation consists in the loosening up of densely built-up areas and the erection of high buildings. This has been called "the discovery of the third dimension," height, as an efficient means of introducing a maximum of air, light, sun, and verdure to previously crowded districts. To every city its pruned Manhattan!

The idea as such is excellent, and its architectural rendering is one of the great architectural contributions of our time, a contribution that cannot be praised too highly. It has laid bare the rottenness of a decaying period of architecture and the hollowness of pseudo modernism—the utmost to which the sterile mind of officials would accommodate itself. Le Corbusier's *Ville Radieuse* will occupy, for a long time to come, the first place among the creations that have opened the way towards the rediscovery of great architecture.

But this plan does not offer a remedy on a large scale for the irrevocable disintegration of our cities. It is cut loose from the forces out of which a new social conscience and a new *élan vital* can grow. Open spaces must be regained by a dispersal of population and industry over wide areas, not by a perpetuation of an even greater concentration within a narrower space. The central open space should be the ideal aim for every city. It would be the diametrical opposite of all former solutions and the constructive beginning of the end of cities.

Skyscrapers, even of a moderate height, can easily house several hundred families. This in itself is not objectionable, but is it a solution that contributes anything toward the overwhelming problem of how a new structure of settlement can be developed? To state these facts is not doing injustice to the architectural merits of the scheme. It is rather a positive assessment, for it may help to remove false expectations that would assign to this concentration in height and area a task it cannot possibly fulfill.

Nor is it a negative criticism to say that these isolated buildings, in spite of their audacity and beauty, are conceived in the same spirit that induces a child to put one brick on the other till it is overjoyed that it can now build higher than before. We have tried to show that we are still very young. Why should we not accept this fact? It is nothing of which we should be ashamed. Rather we should be alive to the challenge of this situation, if we hope to add to the discovery of the third dimension the far greater reality of the fourth dimension, the unity of time and space. The former does not go far enough. It is out of date, like all *bon mots* that are too enthusiastically accepted as revelation.

Persistence in this limited conception leads into an impasse and makes a profound and complex revolution of environment impossible. It may be, however, that we are heading for an ant-State and for an atomization of our individuality. Every obedient citizen would then fulfill with the highest perfection one particular function, and this one function would mean to him the whole life. In such a State tall prisons with innumerable cells, one piled on the other, with numerous gadgets to save time for a delusion of leisure, may be adequate abodes for the functionalized human beings.

I doubt, however, whether these buildings will contribute anything towards social awareness and cultural rejuvenation. They are a courageous revolt against disorder and ugliness and an inspiring document of functional clarity —and yet they are an end, not the prelude to a new era.

In the development of cities two main trends have been operative: one of a general character and the other composed of a number of functional activities which in varying degrees have attracted men to city life.

The general trend is most evidently expressed in the gregarious instinct that lures man away from the country. It is strengthened by the need for political organization and by the desire for an active participation in communal activities or at least a greater nearness to them. In certain periods a greater freedom and a better life are powerful magnets for a migration to the cities. The urge that makes the countryman restless, inducing him to abandon his rural surroundings, is almost as strong as the pull that life in cities exerts on the inarticulate feelings of those for whom the country ceases to be the whole world.

The other trend toward city life includes a variety of causes ranging from communal to individual activities. They may be grouped as follows:

Protection against weather and men
 (oasis towns and fortified places)
Worship (temple and cathedral cities)
Kingship (residence and castle towns)
Politics (administrative centers)
Industry (industrial cities and craftsmen's towns)
Trade (trading and road centers)
Expansion (colonial towns, satellites, new towns)
Reforms (improvement of housing)

Not a single one of all these causes can be regarded as pertaining only to cities, provided that we give up looking at the past for guidance and turn toward the future for inspiration. As a matter of fact, most of these motivations have completely disappeared and the others have lost their one-sided significance. The growth of cities and the growth of civilizations have proceeded simultaneously. This development has come to an end.

Cities are one of the most complex products of every civilization, but they are not the whole and sole expression of the spirit which creates a cultural entity. Cities have been the prime movers of change and expansion all over the world. Now a further expansion of one civilization at the cost of others is impossible. The material and ideal frontiers have been reached, as far as the individual political units are concerned.

This end means also the end of our old concept of the city. Cities are dissolving under the impact of new forces, which, though still fluid, are yet powerful enough to disintegrate the old structure. The material, and above all, the ideal structure of cities is crumbling. An era which has extended over thousands of years is drawing to its close—an era that has seen the slow but irresistible coalescence of civilizations and the ever-increasing concentration of power, wealth, and knowledge in the cities; until today they are flowing over into the country, spreading disorder and ugliness everywhere. They are like giant caravanserais in which the dispossessed proletariat of all classes meets, the professionalized and fractionalized nomads, the slaves of technology, and all those who are haunted by the fear of not being "up to date."

SCALE, SPACE, AND SPRAWL

"No man putteth a piece of new cloth unto an old garment, for that which is put to fill it up taketh away from the garment, and the rent is made worse." This is exactly what is happening today to all cities in all countries. Is it a failure of nerve that prevents us from reshaping our environment and our cities on a large scale, and that makes us believe that we can expect far-reaching results from minor reforms?

The most likely explanation is that living in an age of transition, when old ideas are still powerful and new ideas have not yet sufficiently crystallized to serve as reliable guides, we are perplexed and do not know which way to turn. We feel that our environment is expanding in scope and character, that our mobility is increasing at an unprecedented rate, making distances more and more meaningless, and that the scale of our thinking and acting is widening. At the same time we have to cope with a population explosion and a growing scarcity of space.

This seemingly irreconcilable contradiction between the demands of a widening scale and a contracting space has a disturbing influence upon our decisions. We are torn between the past and the future, between the preservation of what is and the acceptance of what should be, believing that the golden mean is the best and only possible solution of the innumerable problems that impinge upon our cities, making them centers of disorder and frustration.

Goethe's remark on this situation is of particular interest. He said: "when eras are on the decline, all tendencies are subjective; but on the other hand, when matters are ripening for a new epoch, all tendencies are objective."

The scarcity of space is first felt in the cities, and the agents that make this most obvious are the automobiles and the growth of the urban population. The result of this interplay is the chaotic sprawl of the urban agglomerations into the country. It is a general phenomenon that is not restricted to the metropolis and big cities but also affects small towns. The questionable result of this eruption is suburbia, ridiculed and yet regarded by innumerable people as the fulfillment of their fondest dreams. We are hypnotized by this development and are apparently unable or unwilling to stop it.

The interaction between the widening of scale that should direct our action and the contraction of space in and around our cities, created by the increase of population and traffic, has led to a situation where only drastic measures can produce any results—if it is not already too late. It is a very complex problem indeed. It involves not merely suburban sprawl but also the deterioration of the cities proper, the provision of public utilities, including the transportation system, taxation, and the preservation of the countryside.

As in communicating pipes, all these and many more problems have risen to the same level of urgency; a solution is possible only if all are tackled at the same time and with the same intensity. Responsible people know this, and even the private developers may be dimly aware of these difficulties, but nothing decisive is done, at least not in this country, because the only efficient remedy, large-scale planning, violates the most sacred tenets of laissez-faire policy. In order to preserve a freedom that in reality is but a freedom for the few, not for the many, we seem to be ready to put up with even the worst ills of this most admired disorder and to believe that a few administrative adjustments, more highways, and a few minor reforms will remove the causes that have produced these difficulties.

The result of this seemingly inextricable dilemma is a growing frustration and discouragement of the general public. Apathy is spreading, and indecision and vagueness affect the work of city planners. However, this is not their fault.

Rather it is the failure of our civilization to provide the cultural groundwork, the unifying milieu in which the individual will is in unison with the general will and from which cultural creativity and group consciousness have always derived their greatest artistic inspirations.

This cultural humus is lacking, and consequently city officials and city planners are thrown back on their own individual prejudices and predilections. They have hardly any other choice than to experiment with their personal pet theories and to make the best of a bad job. They cannot deliver the right goods because they have not been given the right tools. In many cases they are, therefore, forced to be content with fractional improvements, a few slum clearances, a "prettifying" of squares, or the presentation of showpieces, which may be flattering to the civic pride of the city fathers but which only rarely are of any general importance for the well-being of the citizens. One example may illustrate this trend.

Until the French Revolution cities were homogeneous entities held together by a more or less clear image of society, by a myth built around one focal point. This symbolic and functional center was a temple or a church, a castle or a palace, a city hall or a market. The cities that developed around these centers were small and compact, with easy personal contact and little traffic. Proximity made unity of the functional and personal life immediate and realistic.

All these trends developed and were conceived and adapted for functions and a style of life totally different from our own. But the idea of the city center has lived on, although it has lost its functional and symbolic significance. As a matter of fact, the renewal or the preservation of the core has become the pet ambition of numerous mayors and their city-planning advisors. They seem to be insensitive to the grave complications that this policy involves.

Ever more and higher buildings are pressed into the already overcrowded central district. New garages are erected, attracting an ever-growing number of automobiles. New expressways to the core district are planned or built. More and more shops are opened, eager to make the most of this favorable opportunity of the concentration of large numbers of potential customers within a small area. But the limited space available for this increasing influx of cars and people has grown so cluttered, and attempts to disentangle the congestion are so inefficient, that it seems impossible to bring the situation under control.

It is more than doubtful that elevated access roads to the center will solve the problem in the long run. Moreover, this "solution" is not applicable in most city centers: the building density is too high and it is impossible to cut through the solid mass of buildings without a very far-reaching demolition that is, in any case, too expensive. The causes, not the symptoms, should be attacked. Only a radical loosening up of the core can hold out any hope of lasting improvement. But old habits and ideas die slowly. It is one of the major deceptions to assume that the old circular structure of cities, this legacy of the past, of the walled-in towns, has ceased to exist. It is still there, physically and socially, though it has grown amorphous.

The central city is surrounded by the inner rings of the substandard quarters. Then follow the zone of the nondescript so-called better residential districts, and finally the suburbs. Beyond these rings are the outlying towns, gradually sinking to the level of satellites the more the big cities expand and fortify their role as competitors.

Every central city is a dead weight on the social and economic body of an urban community. It is kept going by values of property, rents, profits, and taxes. And the people who keep it going are property owners, mostly absentee landlords, politicians and administrators, and commercial institutions. There is something fundamentally wrong with our central cities. It is a symbol of the first order that many of the central districts are deserted during the night. The City of London is perhaps the most characteristic example.

We will return to the role of the core district in relation to regional planning in the next part. Here it may be sufficient to condense the problem in one sentence: as long as children have to play in dirty and dangerous streets, and as long as great numbers of the population have to live in slums, however much their "intimacy" and their "warmth and immediacy of human relations" are praised by a few incorrigible romantics, no responsible city-planning official should lend a hand or give a thought to making the city center a showpiece of his city.

What has been done or is planned in some of the great metropolises of the world to cope with the growing pressure of population and with the increasing scarcity of space? Let us examine, in broad outline, London, Paris, Tokyo, Washington, and New York, the city without a plan.

London.   The Greater London Plan of 1944 provided for moving out more than one million people to new towns, housing estates, and other communities beyond the green belt, and for redeveloping the central district of London. This attempt was partly successful. The number of residents has decreased by about one million and there are about half a million fewer factory jobs in the metropolitan area, but office and service jobs have increased, canceling out the gains in other fields. Today more people than ever before work in London and come in from greater distances.

Beyond the green belt, the population of the outer urban ring is increasing by more than 100,000 annually, at five times the national average. It has been estimated that in two decades this outer urban ring will be one continuous zone of settlement, with more than two million people living and working in it, and that the open country will be pushed back beyond the outer edge of this urbanized girdle. By that time London will have spread over almost the whole of southeast England, over 5,000 square miles, to the coasts of Sussex, Kent, and Essex. With this expansion all public services will be strained beyond capacity, because the hundreds of millions for extension and improvement will not be available.

As the capital and cultural hub of the nation, as the largest port, and the center of the transportation system, of business and entertainment, and as the principal industrial city, apart from heavy industries and textiles, the attraction of London will continue undiminished. But the government's attitude, lacking vision and courage, is ambivalent: on the one hand, it pays lip service to decentralization, and on the other it furthers the erection of large office buildings in London and seems to give its blessings to the rebuilding of Covent Garden market in the central area. Its powers to direct (not merely to "guide") industries into other regions are insufficient, and it is most likely that they will remain so for decades.

So far the concept of redevelopment on a large scale is a parody of what it could and should be: it is restricted to a minor relocation of factories and houses without a simultaneous cultural decentralization—the typical and sterile half-measures of a policy of muddling through. The only efficient solution would be a national plan for the whole country. But this possibility, which was seriously discussed in the immediate postwar years, is dismissed as "unrealistic" by the so-called *Realpolitiker,* who for fear of the new and unusual cling with all their might to the old, although they should know that history has always proved them wrong in the end. New satellite towns and the green belt are the response of England to the challenge of the metropolis.

Paris.   The development of metropolitan Paris has released a lively controversy between a group of architects and the government. The architects propose a *Paris Parallele* to relieve the pressure upon the suburban growth of the capital—a second city separated from the old by a green belt. The Committee of Architects declared: "In our opinion only *Paris Parallele,* new city of the twentieth century, offers the radical, efficient, logical and economic solution to the problem of the capital. Only it is worthy of France." The old and the new Paris would be connected by a superhighway leading through the forest-like barrier of the green belt.

The government plan is conservative and formalistic. It suggests that the suburban zone should be redeveloped but not extended, and that a number of "subcities" should be built around Paris, with secondary centers between them and other communities at a great distance linked to the "subcities." This network of communities centered on Paris would relieve, the government hopes, the pressure on Paris proper.

This scheme could have been devised by a military engineer, who surrounded his central fortress with outlying forts and strongpoints, all interconnected by underground passages. Perhaps the spirit of the old fortress of Paris has been the godparent to this plan. The response of France to the challenge of the metropolis is either a new city or satellite towns.

Tokyo.   The population of Tokyo has hit the nine-million mark and is increasing at the rate of about two to three hundred thousand each year. It is highly improbable that this growth can or will be checked in the near future. It is the outcome of a long-established tendency of centralization that seems to be deeply rooted in historical and social conditions. If this trend continues, the population of Tokyo may reach fifteen million in twenty years.

What will the "Tokyo of tomorrow" be like? Two plans are proposed. One envisages that the vast area of the Kanto Plain, with Tokyo as its center, should be rationally planned; the other proposes the reclamation of the Bay of Tokyo and the building on the new land of a second Tokyo. A certain similarity with the two plans for Paris is obvious.

The land-based scheme is more matter of fact and orthodox and was advocated earlier, shortly after the war. Its main suggestions are: a green belt around the existing city that would check its growth, and a number of satellite towns on the Kanto Plain connected with Tokyo and with each other by high-speed transportation.

The reclamation plan has stimulated an enormous interest among the citizens of Tokyo. It has been rightly asked, If the Zuider Zee has been reclaimed, why not Tokyo Bay? There is, however, one possible obstacle that has to be given serious consideration: the probable weakness of the reclaimed ground against earthquakes.

The central idea of this scheme is to reclaim an area greater than the whole of Tokyo today and to build a new second Tokyo on this new land "along the most modern lines." It was first ventilated in 1958. Then it was taken up by a committee of business leaders and numerous experts and published in 1959 as "Recommendation concerning the Filling-up of Tokyo Bay" and addressed by the Industrial Planning Conference to the government and the general public.

This *Neo Tokyo Plan* provides, as the first stage, for the reclamation of 400 million square meters along the margins of Tokyo Bay—a work that would take fifteen to twenty years. When a further 200 million square meters have been reclaimed, about two-thirds of the Bay will have been converted into land. The cost for the entire reclamation work has been estimated at about 3.8 million yen (1 dollar=358.70 yen).

Of the total population within the Tokyo area, which will have risen to over fourteen million in 1975, about three million will be accommodated in the Tokyo-Yokohama area and another 2,700,000 in the Tokyo-Chiba area. In both cases large industrial zones will occupy the greater part of the newly reclaimed land, while residential districts will spread over the hills in the background. Large open spaces are to be reserved for parks, airfields, and so on. Commercial establishments, government offices, and the like are also to be located in the new city. About 30 per cent of the reclaimed land is reserved for highways and roads, a considerably bigger proportion than the former of only 10 per cent.

Water supply, previously mainly from underground sources, had the disadvantage of causing subsidence of the ground and damage to buildings. Studies are being made of the Tone River, flowing through the Kanto Plain and, if it proves possible, water will be supplied from this source.

The reaction to this plan was divided. All shades of opinion were represented, varying from enthusiastic acceptance to skeptical indecision and outright rejection. A Tokyo newspaper, *Asahi,* raised a strong and justified objection in an article published on August 3, 1959:

The plan to fill up Tokyo Bay has as its base a nonchalance as to the extensive concentration of population in Tokyo. A population that will almost double in twenty years is to be dumped into a new city built in Tokyo Bay. This looks, at the first glance, like a positive policy but will hardly avoid the reproach of violating a fundamental principle of metropolitan redevelopment. Taking industry as an example it may be doubted whether such a concentration in Tokyo will be advisable or not. Is it not more proper to distribute industry more evenly over Japan and to encourage simultaneously industrial and economic development throughout the country?

Nothing need be added to this criticism. The response of Japan to the challenge of megalopolis is, in either case, the land-based or the reclamation scheme, heavily tinged with the adoration of giantism. But in this respect Japan is not a lone wanderer in the wilderness of misguided ambitions.

Washington, D.C.   About two million people are now living in the Greater Washington area. By the turn of the century the population may have increased to five million. The new plan, which was published in 1961, proposes a starlike development with corridors extending out from the present urban core, each composed of a number of communities linked together along six radial highways with rapid transit lines. At the same time the interior of the city would be developed to emphasize "the monument image" of Washington, to provide more open spaces, and to make the Capitol more distinctive.

Other plans were also under consideration: new cities about seventy miles from the central city; new towns, each absorbing 50,000 to 150,000 people, distributed throughout the area, and an enlargement of the central urban mass; a ring of smaller new towns, each with a population of 50,000 to 80,000, sited regularly at a distance of about thirty miles and absorbing up to 7,500,000 people; or a concentric suburban zone with self-sufficient communities of about 100,000 persons each, not separated from the metropolitan area.

Washington is, of course, a special case. It is not an industrial city or a metropolis in the strict sense of London, Paris, or Tokyo. In this respect it is almost unique, comparable only to cities such as Canberra, Ankara, or Brasilia, although these are too new and do not have the same symbolic prominence. As the political and administrative capital of the nation, its life has a distinguished character of its own. A development plan should, therefore, be based on a concept very different from the usual procedure.

It may still be too early to form a definite judgment in this respect, but it would appear that underlying the present plan there is the tacit assumption that this unique city has, like other cities, the mission to grow, and that a prevention of this growth would mean stagnation. Why this should be so is, to say the least, open to doubt. A considerable number of government offices could be distributed just as easily as industrial or commercial offices are without any damage to the efficiency of the administration.

The cancer of Bigness should not be allowed to develop in an urban body of one of the few nonindustrial cities of the world that has retained a high degree of individuality. Thus, the final response to the unique challenge of the particular character of Washington may still be in the balance, fluctuating between conventional lines and the search for an unorthodox solution more in keeping with the original intention of L'Enfant.

New York. This city without a plan will have within

its region by 1985 a population of twenty-two million. I hesitate to write down what my personal feelings are about the results of the "planning for chaos" that allowed New York to grow like a malignant tumor, affecting the whole body of the metropolitan region. After all, my own feelings are irrelevant in this respect, and not important enough to be advertised.

I prefer, therefore, to quote just a few sentences taken at random from Raymond Vernon's *Metropolis 1985*, the synthesis of a comprehensive survey of the metropolitan area. If nothing is done to stop the present development and direct it into the right channels, the future will see: "a region developing thinly and patchily at the edges. . . the eating-up of open space. . . a profligate, planless use of the land. . . reduced hopes of capturing large tracts for recreational purposes, little consideration of traffic implications. . . continual rise of incompatible uses of contiguous land."

Much more could be added, but these few observations, which touch some of the sorest points of the metropolitan malady, may be sufficient to show the danger of a policy that allows private enterprise to run amok. The outward trend that increases from year to year does not relieve the inner congestion. It merely absorbs the new influx into the region.

Ever more people are packed into the core area, and one opportunity after the other to preserve or re-create open spaces for recreation and to loosen up the congestion is missed. Welfare Island in the East River is a case in point: 70,000 people are to be settled there in high apartment blocks raised on platforms, under which, one may suppose, Nature is permitted to give a faint sign of existence.

What is the response to the tremendous challenge of the New York megalopolis? The answer is plain and simple: none—or perhaps the same that has been said of Welfare

Island: to use "the most valuable piece of undeveloped real estate in the world."

All these examples have in common the fact that their development plans (or unchecked trends, as in New York) are focused on an existing central city, even in the case of *Paris Parallele* and *Neo Tokyo*. None even tries to ventilate the possibility of a far-reaching dispersal that would help to eliminate, or at least to reduce, the causes of the only too obvious problems.

They are all restricted to a treatment of the symptoms, hoping against hope that the grafting-on of a few new parts will remedy the situation. None of these plans attempts to reshape the physical structure on a large scale, but all succumb to the views of giantism. This superpragmatic and yet at the same time almost fatalistic attitude can only lead to disaster.

Let me conclude this chapter by repeating some of the words that Botero wrote in 1606 in his *Treatise Concerning the Causes of the Magnificence and Greatness of Cities*:

Let no man think that a city may go on in increase without ceasing. . . . The ordinary greatness of a city depends upon remote causes and cannot long endure. For every man will seek his commodities and ease where he may find it best.

chapter three

LIVING SPACE

FOR THE

NEW MILLIONS

O<small>UR</small> environment is expanding, but the interplay of space, scale, and sprawl continues to spread disorder
over ever-larger regions and growing spheres of urban and
rural existence. No determined attempts have been made to
cope with this situation on a large scale through a systematic physical and cultural decentralization and dispersal of
the congested conurbations. The outburst into the wide unexplored spaces of the world, which in the Renaissance
heralded the beginning of a new age, is repeated today with
far greater intensity in scope and character.

To conquer space, to explore the universe, are realizable
ambitions of mankind. New energies are released. A new
vision of life is born, and with it a keen awareness of un-

limited possibilities takes hold of the mind of an ever-growing number of people. Just as in the Renaissance the discovery of new lands and new inventions transformed the attitude to life and left its mark on all works of man, on the urban and rural environment, so today the impact of the emerging possibilities will revolutionize our environment more fundamentally than at any other period of history, with the exception of the agricultural and urban revolutions.

It is a great demand that is made upon us. Many cherished ideas will have to be discarded. New ideals have to be evolved and absorbed: and although it is not too likely that the Malthusian problem will be solved by interstellar migrations, the imagination, the power, and the enthusiasm that are the agents of this outward drive into the universe cannot fail to reshape the scale and the character of our terrestial actions.

But apart from these considerations, there are very cogent and practical reasons that should make us pause for reflection. The most obvious reason is the population explosion. Where will the new millions live and how will they be accommodated? In cities, even if the urban environment is improved?

The scriptural injunction, "Increase and multiply," is no longer a sensible proposition. The world population is now exceeding 2.7 billion and doubling about every fifty years. The present rate of increase, of 1 per cent per year, is rising, and according to the demographic estimates of the United Nations will have reached 3 per cent by the year 2000.

About 10,000 years ago the total population of the world engaged in hunting and food gathering may have been something over five million. After the agricultural revolution and in the early stages of the urban revolution the total had exceeded eighty-six million. At the time of Christ it had risen to perhaps 250 million. The first doubling to 500 million took 1,600 years; the next doubling to one billion only 250 years, in 1850; the third doubling to two billion only eighty years, in 1930. If the present trends continue, the total population will have reached four billion in the late 1970's—a doubling in about forty years—and over six billion by 2000.

Population growth is most rapid in the underdeveloped countries, in Asia, Latin America, and most of Africa, where about two-thirds of the world's population live in conditions that are near or below the subsistence minimum. If this development persists unchecked, it will divide the world even more sharply than political rivalries into two antagonistic groups: the "have" and the "have-not" blocs. This is the over-all picture.

In this country, the United States, there will be more than 300 million by 2000, but this prospect does not seem to provoke serious thought on the environmental problems which this increase will create. David Riesman remarks on this attitude of the younger American generation in *Problems of United States Economic Development,* The Committee for Economic Development:

Serious discussion of the future is just what is missing in the United States. . . . We live now, think later. . . . I think we fear opacity of the future, and try not to pierce it with concrete plans. . . . What we fear to face is more than total destruction; it is total meaninglessness.

This attitude will not solve the problems of the urban and suburban chaos nor will it help to revitalize the rural areas. The population of the U.S.S.R. was, at the beginning of 1959, according to the All-Union census, somewhat over 208 million, and the natural increase exceeded 3½ million per year. The urban population had risen from 60.4 million before the war to almost 100 million in 1959, and the number of cities and urban-type settlements from 2,759 in 1939 to 4,616 in 1959.

This increase continued up to the initiation of the Virgin Lands Program in 1954; then it began to decline and the population in the eastern areas increased by 16 million, a trend that is likely to continue. Although the rate of growth of the urban population is very considerable, it seems that great efforts are being made to settle large numbers of the population in rural areas—an effort that, if successful, would reduce the pressure on the cities.

China is in a different position. Of its almost 650 million people, a majority live in rural areas. By 1955 about 100 million lived in cities, a number that has risen during the last years. China has twenty-five cities with a population of more than 500,000, but the bulk of the urban population lives in small market towns. Nearly 75 per cent of the total population are concentrated in 15 per cent of the national territory, in the eastern lowlands and hills, and in Szechwan, the most populous province.

These three countries represent three different types of population problems, but have in common the pressure of a growing population upon the urban areas and on the available space in general. India and Pakistan are in positions not too dissimilar to that of China. It would go far beyond the scope of this work to go into a detailed investigation of their national differences. The most threatening problem is everywhere the same: the population explosion forces a new assessment of how the new millions—in some cases also the old millions—can be settled and housed in a dignified manner that will disperse the vast urban conglomerations and create a balanced structure of settlement over the whole national territory.

DECENTRALIZATION
AND DISPERSAL

The goal of a new structure of settlement is not to change the urbanite into a suburbanite. Nor is it anything like the production of numerous blueprints for new communities, green belts, parkways, and rural areas—possibilities only discussed among those who fail to understand that life cannot be pressed into the strait jacket of preconceived schemes or narrow ideas. The large-scale and long-term plans that are needed cannot be anything else but a flexible framework for future action. But what should be absolutely clear is the direction in which we intend to move ahead, and the delineation of those areas which are to be thinned out and those which are to be developed. Furthermore, if we want to create a dynamic equilibrium of settlement, we should think and act in processes, not according to notions of static entities. How can we proceed?

In broad terms our task is threefold: the replacement of the built-up areas which are "lost" through the thinning-out and through the reduction of population and building density in the cities, the conversion of hitherto undeveloped or not fully developed areas into living space for the new millions, and an organic integration of the old and the new areas over large regions. The guiding principles to achieve these goals are decentralization and dispersal. The instruments are city, regional, and national planning.

Decentralization and dispersal are interdependent. They affect urban and rural areas alike. Decentralization should be understood not in the narrower sense of a decentralization of industry but in its broader meaning of decentralization of settlement, that is, the loosening up of urban districts. Dispersal, on the other hand, spreads beyond the confines of the area from which the overflow of population is to be drained. Thus, decentralization proceeds within a narrower space than dispersal; and dispersal begins where decentralization ends.

Decentralization remains focused on a center. It is a procedure that does not diminish the importance of the center as such, but changes the spatial structure and interdependence and the functions radiating from it within its sphere of influence. Dispersal affects more or less widely separated places and areas and creates new mental and material relationships to a new environment. A clear distinction between both these principles is essential, if the different types of planning are not to be confused and are to serve as really efficient instruments. Both, decentralization and dispersal, have a dual effect: they influence the places, districts, and regions from which people migrate and those to which they move.

Decentralization is a term much used—and misused—today. Its equivalent on the Continent is the German term *Entballung der Staedte,* the decongestion of cities. The problem is the same everywhere, and, unfortunately, the resulting misunderstandings are also identical. Decentralization, as it is mostly understood, is the development of suburbs on the fringes of the central city, which is preserved as substantially the same compact entity that it has been before: the all-absorbing and domineering influence on the life of the decentralized units.

This "decentralization," however, has nothing to do with an organic decentralization that affects the core city and its surroundings at the same time and with the same intensity. It does not lead to a systematic loosening up of the over-crowded urban areas, nor does it lead to a balanced physical, social and economic integration of the metropolitan area.

The instruments of planning are, as mentioned above, city, regional, and national planning. These are interdependent, like decentralization and dispersal, and should be used simultaneously or the results will be a patchwork of un-related reforms that, after a short time, will be more difficult to improve than the present situation.

In order to forestall wrong expectations and to clarify the exact objectives of this investigation, it may be pertinent to repeat that in this connection it is neither possible nor de-sirable to produce a manual of city planning, a sort of "do-it-yourself" pamphlet on how to proceed. Here we are ex-clusively concerned with the methods in general, how they should be applied, and what the results should be. And further: the aim is the transformation of the urban and rural environment on a large scale through the redistribution of the fundamental needs of homes, work, distribution and cir-culation, leisure and recreation, social intercourse, and cul-tural stimulation.

And finally, I want to confute one argument that is, as I know from experience, most likely to be put forward, namely, that the following suggestions are basically not dif-ferent from the usual plans for the decentralization of urban areas. To the best of my knowledge, there is not one single proposition that tries to eliminate the traditional role of the city as an all-absorbing center. All proposals, even if they envisage a fairly far-reaching decentralization, leave the

central city intact and maintain its spirit and its co1 ʔ. Frank
Lloyd Wright's *The Disappearing City* comes, perhaps,
nearer to the ideas propounded in this work, although they
have not been thought out and worked out in intelligible
form.

I do not pretend for a moment that my own ideas offer
a final solution or that they cannot be criticized on any
reasonable ground. On the contrary, I hope that they will
stimulate discussion and reassessment. But I do maintain
that they deviate fundamentally from all the patterns which
have been suggested as possible city development, be they
stars or fingers, wedges or rings, galaxies or a combination
of several of these pattern-book models.

For me, and many like-minded people, the twilight of
cities is a fact, and I cannot convince myself that it is possible or useful to revive something that is dead, namely, the
city. I have to rely on the indulgence of the reader, "your
humble patience, pray," if I venture once more to ask for
his objective and unbiased reflection on my insistence that
the starting point of the following proposal is not city renewal but city dispersal. It may be that my ideas fall short
of the expectations I have raised and that the last remarks
are regarded as an expression of apologetic diffidence. The
first may be true; the second is definitely not.

City or Local Planning

This procedure generates centrifugal tendencies and
furthers existing trends working in the same direction. The
process is reversed: in the past centripetal forces formed and
sustained the urban structure even where cities expanded or
grew amorphous at the periphery.

This new type of city planning aims at a radical thinning-out of the total urban area through population movement, and transfer of activities and buildings and equipment to other places, which regional or national schemes, or both, have assigned as suitable locations for similar functions in the new structure of settlement. This is the program. The *methods* to realize it are:

1. No slums are to be rebuilt; the areas gained by slum clearance are to be retained as open spaces.

2. The core of the urban area is to be loosened up by the evacuation of commercial enterprises, entertainment and cultural institutions, and small industries located in the central area, gradually increasing in scope and intensity till the densely built-up area is converted into a central open space.

3. The open spaces thus gained are to be interrelated as a continuous park system connecting the former slums, the central open space, and the thinned-out residential quarters and industrial districts. Gradually this will turn what has been a congested urban area into a park landscape merging into the open country.

Slum Clearance.   Slums cannot be demolished before new accommodation is available and industries and white-collar jobs are redistributed through regional allocation. Consequently, slum clearance and dispersal of the core areas are a combined operation. The areas reclaimed in this process may be small and widely dispersed, sometimes consisting of only a few isolated plots. Nevertheless, they form the original nuclei of the comprehensive scheme of dispersal. In the beginning they may serve as neighborhood playgrounds or recreation areas that can easily be prepared for this purpose.

As provisional amenities they do not involve a major expenditure.

The Urban Core.   It has been mentioned above that the scarcity of space is felt first in the cities. It may, therefore, seem to be absurd to suggest a further reduction of space exactly in the area where congestion is greatest. To define this procedure in these terms is, of course, self-contradictory because the causes that have produced the congestion—buildings and streets—are removed and the area previously confined by them is converted into an open space. In other words, the space needed for these buildings, streets, and squares is shifted to other places within the regional scheme.

In general, urban centers are to be redeveloped as central open spaces and not to be rebuilt. After all, as has been explained on the foregoing pages, there is no need to preserve these overgrown tumors in the centers of cities. They are a disturbing legacy of the past, dating back to the Middle Ages.

There is no justification for retaining the concentration of offices and shops in the heart of the urban communities—especially not now, when the cities are spilling over into the countryside and when these concentrations are the main reason why all our cities suffer from an accelerated arteriosclerosis and stagnation. Shopping centers, with a great variety of shops and even with opportunities for specialized shopping, are moving out to the suburbs. Economic activities are redistributed from the older central districts to the fringe areas; retail trades, household services, warehousing, and other industrial services follow the same trend.

In a study, *Guiding Metropolitan Growth,* made by the Committee for Economic Development in 1960, this outward movement has been investigated in detail, although the recommendations advocated in this statement on national policy maintain the essential principles of metropolitan growth.

Of thirteen million dwelling units erected in nonfarm areas from 1946 through 1958, approximately eleven million, or 85 per cent, have been located outside central cities. Both sales and jobs in retail lines have dropped steadily in the core as a proportion of the New York region over a 25-year period with the outer rings registering the corresponding gains. . . . A gradual but unremitting relative decline in manufacturing jobs located in central cities is also discernible. [On the other hand] certain types of activities show little inclination to deconcentrate. Business and governmental services requiring face-to-face relationships or dependence upon a large pool of female labour continue to exercise a strong preference for office space in the core of large metropolitan areas.

This latter conclusion may be correct for the time being, that is, within the present structure of settlement, but there is no reason to assume that this will not or cannot change in different conditions. Face-to-face relationships are more and more replaced by telephone or other media of communication, and grow increasingly impersonal the more the trend toward the organized irresponsibility of committees or of large trusts becomes the order of the day.

Then there are the "gray areas" between the business core and the suburbs, where in the first quarter of this century the majority of families lived. Since 1945 the exodus from these areas has gathered momentum, and lower income groups, including racial minorities, have moved into these potential slums.

Industries, especially those producing standardized goods, are shifting to horizontal-line processing in one-story plants and are thus forced out of the crowded districts to larger sites outside the urban areas where industrial districts or trading estates can be developed.

Taking all these movements together, there is a definite "natural" trend away from the core of cities. A determined prompting and persuasion is, therefore, not out of place and would ultimately produce results which are already in the making.

However, old ideas and habits die hard. It is not surprising to observe that city centers are treated in development plans almost as a Holy of Holies. They seem to be sacrosanct, and not only their existence but also their expansion are taken for granted. The possibility of reducing the central conglomerations never enters the minds of planning officials. They rationalize *ex post facto* what they believe to be the only "reasonable" solution, without even faintly realizing that there may be other ideas that should at least be investigated. Their attitude is reminiscent of Christian Morgenstern's Palmström, when after a street accident, in which he was knocked down by a car, he concludes *"dass nicht sein kann, was nicht sein darf."**

In this mood they lay down the law that a "vital" center will continue to exist and to develop as the decision making area of a metropolis. But why is it "vital"? Is decision-making an activity that must be concentrated in the center? True, it may affect a majority of citizens, but only a relatively small number are needed to make decisions. Moreover, in this affluent society an ever growing number of urbanites are contracting out of active participation in politics, because they know from experience that their vote has no

---

* In a free translation this means: "that nothing can be that ought not to be".

purpose other than to enable the various parties to play musical chairs, and that the new team forgets only too easily the promises made during the election campaign. This may be regrettable, but it can certainly not be altered by concentrating decision-making in the central city.

Why do city planning officials assume as an undeniable fact that the trend towards greater need for office space will continue? Of course, it will continue, if no other opportunities are offered elsewhere. I believe that it is almost impossible to argue with planners who are overwhelmed by the pressure of daily routine work and are not free to propose more radical changes or to convince the city fathers that this preservation of the *status quo*, even with some modifications, is unrealistic.

Traffic congestion will increase if retail trades and cultural activities continue to be packed together in the core area. This approach will not solve the problem. It is a retrogressive "solution" that will make matters worse. It retains basically the concentric development of the urban area, and prefers a static pattern to an organic and linear decentralization.

The central open space would eliminate the most disturbing features of urban congestion and of a deceptive urban attraction. It would revitalize the communal structure and create a focal area that is the real property of all inhabitants, their genuine community center, which the park system spreads to all parts of the region.

Only a small number of the activities previously concentrated in the core city are to be grouped together within a small area. This would include certain branches of the administration and possibly some headquarters of large commercial enterprises. A careful investigation would have to precede the selection of the institutions that would qualify for a location in a relatively narrow compass. They would form the *Desk City,* empty at night and used only in daytime. This City can be located at the fringes of the central park, loosely laid out with ample open spaces, underground access roads, and garages.

Parks and Parkways. The grid of parks and parkways is the first prerequisite for a rational tidying up of the whole amorphous urban mass. A green belt, or green islands interspersed between the built-up areas, or green wedges penetrating to the center from the periphery are insufficient means to achieve this end. Nature should be omnipresent, not merely as a Sunday amenity but as an indispensable part of everyday life, on the daily walks to the schools, to the shopping centers, to the stations, and to other parts of the community.

The atmosphere, the mental and sentimental influence of our environment, can create conditions that are essential to our well-being, even more essential than the satisfaction of our material needs. Verdure not only within easy reach but within direct view of every inhabitant resembles the keynote of a polyphonic composition. Every settlement of the future should be a park community. Even the industrial districts, with the possible exception of those for heavy industry, can be made partners in this revolution of environment, situated in green surroundings near playing fields and in direct connection with the open landscape.

The realization of this goal would be the final fulfillment of the hopeful beginning inaugurated over two hundred years ago by John Wood's plan for Bath. His plan marked the end of an era which excluded Nature from the built-up urban areas. In Bath this principle was abandoned. The architects opened their town to the open country. They built the new quarters on the hilly slopes of the surrounding land and made Nature an essential element of the whole. With this decision modern city planning was born. It is left to us to draw the ultimate conclusions from this sublime example—not only in theory but in practice. The far-reaching integration of Nature with architecture has a profound effect on the structure and atmosphere of the community.

It creates—	*It rejects—*
A unifying element.	Piecemeal incoherence.
A stimulus to the dramatization of social life and the revivification of individual life.	Self-centered insensibility.

It generates—	*It ends—*
A spill-over of the population into the region.	Overcrowding and high density.
A direct interaction between the region and the urban area.	Disfiguration and misuse of the countryside by urban sprawl.
Intimate awareness by the townspeople of the cycle of Nature.	Antagonism between city and country.

It produces—	*It abolishes—*
A loosening up of the block system.	Rigidity.
A splitting up of the block front.	Uniformity.
A disintegration of the speculative lot system.	Cut-to-pattern buildings.

It provides—	*It prevents—*
A steady flow of fresh air.	Stagnation and pollution of the air.
Free access to sun and light.	Sunless and drab rooms.
An easy opportunity for recreation.	Indoor rustiness.

It enforces—	*It avoids—*
Diversity of layout and buildings.	Repetition.
Regeneration of architecture and space relations.	Traditional humbug.
Reorganization of traffic.	Stop-gap modifications.

The character of the streets will gradually change. Instead of dull and uniform canyons, the streets will be open ribbons, rhythmically articulated by groups of buildings with free views to other parts of the community. The uninterrupted walls of houses, the continuous block fronts, will disappear. Traffic arteries will be so laid out that they only skirt the communities, never passing through any urban or rural settlement. Consequently, they will no longer converge on a center, the less so as central areas have ceased to exist as attracting focal points. Secondary access roads will lead to the residential and industrial districts, providing a grid of communications over the whole area.

The separation of fast traffic from residential, recreational, and working district, and the organic direction of local traffic with a minimum of interference in all those areas where the pedestrian is king, not the automobile, restore to life one of the most essential elements which lift it above the level of a narrow parochialism: mobility, a possibility that everyone wants to exploit and to enjoy, that has been lost in the chaos of our congested cities and highways. We shall deal with this problem later in detail.

Some general observations may clarify the consequences of the ideas put forward on the foregoing pages. Physical dispersal without a simultaneous cultural dispersal leads nowhere. It would make all efforts illusory, and maintain the old-fashioned unity by centralization instead of creating integration by organic dispersal over a wide area. The new mobility enables us to reexamine the need for a concentration of cultural institutions in the most populous communities.

What cultural opportunities can be offered as public services? I am not referring to the inevitable second- and third-rate cinemas and other commercialized entertainments that cater to the lower level of uncritical enjoyment. The cultural media that provide for enrichment and creative development of the mind belong to another category. In this connection I am thinking exclusively of those institutions which can give a distinctive character to a community and whose formative and attracting power is strong enough to radiate over a wide area.

To this group belong all educational services, such as universities and colleges, libraries, opportunities for adult enlightenment, and, of course, schools, which are in any case dispersed all over the country. Furthermore, there are museums, exhibitions, theaters, concert halls, and other similar opportunities. All the cultural goods these institutions can provide are mobile. There is no need whatsoever to regard them as "fixed industries" that must be located in only a few big cities.

In the new structure of settlement there may be university towns similar to those which already exist, as, for instance, Princeton, Oxford, and Cambridge, but of a purer character, not spoilt by the encroachment of industries. There may be places where theater and opera performances imprint their mark on the life of the community. There may be museum towns from which traveling exhibitions are regularly sent out. There may be festival towns where special entertainments are organized. The rudiments of this dispersal do exist, and it is necessary only to evolve them further and to get rid of the notion that most of these opportunities should be concentrated in one or several big cities.

None of these institutions, let us repeat, is fixed to one place, but each can be made the focal point of the communal life of a small community. Their accessibility will be improved because our mobility is increased. To drive to a place, say, 20 or 30 miles away, over first-rate roads will take less time than to squeeze through traffic jams, to stop at innumerable red lights, and to face the almost insuperable problem of parking.

Would it not be an exciting adventure to lift the visit to a museum or a theater out of the routine of everyday life by surrounding it with the atmosphere of a festive occasion, and to attend a performance or look at works of art in a setting of natural beauty, instead of in an environment that makes relaxation impossible, whose noise and smell impair concentration and enjoyment? Is the popularity of open-air performances not perhaps an indication of this desire for a more stimulating environment?

In any case, the dispersal of cultural amenities to small communities is justified for two reasons: their removal from the hustle and bustle of the big cities and the need to make them revitalizing factors of the life of small communities. Their creative effectiveness will increase because they are more easily accessible and, above all, because the atmosphere surrounding them radiates the special attraction of something unusual.

It is astonishing to observe how strongly city planners are influenced by stereotyped patterns of urban development. The past and theoretical rigidity make them insensitive to the potentialities inherent in our situation. Virtually all metropolitan development schemes are based on the preservation of a city center, even if a far-reaching decentralization is suggested. The patterns for this decentralization are more or less the time-honored stars or rings or similar figures. A particularly ingenious city planner has even promoted the idea of a shifting center that would wander with the extension of the city.

This *idée fixe* has taken such a hold over their minds that they fail to see the great possibilities a flexible and unbiased approach to the reshaping of our environment offers. They cannot shed the notion of metropolitan growth, as though a metropolis or a big city is something permanent, something unique that is not subject to fundamental change. Change is permanent, however, not cities, and this change can be sometimes violent and most destructive, if it is not voluntarily and in time brought under control.

The advocates of urban supremacy are apparently convinced that metropolitan existence will be the normal way of life in the future. This may or may not be so. Looking at the world today, we can see ourselves heading for an ant-state, and a decaying urban civilization spreading over our planet in spite of, or just because of, its inner contradictions.

If this is what the exponents of an unmitigated urbanization expect, would it not be more reasonable to try to remedy the causes, instead of treating the symptoms with small doses of homeopathic drugs, such as drawing-board patterns of layout or lovely clover-leaves and similar patent medicines? Why does this school of thought assume that a systematic and large-scale dispersion would make easy accessibility to rural land unnecessary and would impair spontaneous communication and choice of residence? Why would small communities have a high density at the center and why would the flow of activities and traffic converge at the center of each community? On what grounds can small communities that have come into existence in an organic regional development be equated with satellite towns in the usual sense, or, by implication, can only a metropolis be "imaginable" and not dispersed small communities? And why is the encouragement of continued metropolitan agglomerations accepted as the gospel of city planning? Why are all these assumptions put forward as guiding principles of city planning?

The answer is simple: it is contained in the tacit postulate of continued metropolitan agglomeration. I do not want to repeat the arguments against this policy, but I do believe that this approach to the grave problems of an unchecked urbanization is not only sterile but dangerous, and that the danger, which inevitably will grow in intensity, can be avoided by a determined turning away from outworn doctrines and a serious search for solutions more attuned to the future.

Regional Planning

Looked at from the vantage point of our present situation, in this case from the existing cities, regional planning exerts a pull away from the urban areas, while within the region it tends towards concentration and interdependence of hitherto more or less isolated settlement units. Although this is perhaps too doctrinaire and theoretical an explanation, it may help to clarify the difference between city and regional planning.

Before we proceed to define the meaning and purpose of regional planning, a few words on metropolitan planning may be pertinent. I have often been asked what is the difference between city and metropolitan planning. My answer has always been: none—metropolitan planning merely covers a larger area but works on the same erroneous principles and uses the same methods. Metropolitan planning, as understood in this country, is mostly concerned with some administrative or organizational adjustments or, at best, with the preservation of open spaces. It does not, or if at all, only very timidly, try to interfere with the mushroom growth of suburbs or similar outlying excrescences of the metropolis.

Moreover, the term metropolitan planning is often mixed up with "regional" planning, thus confusing the issues even more. What is meant by this terminology is merely the metropolitan region, which is in any case a rather elusive something. Metropolitan planning should disappear from the vocabulary and the program of work of city planners and be made part and parcel of genuine regional planning. It could have been useful if it had at least begun to introduce some order into the chaotic mess of urban sprawl and to develop a system of functional spacing as the first step toward an organic redistribution of settlement and industry. This opportunity has passed. The metropolitan tentacles are grabbing more and more land.

An alleviation of this unrestricted absorption of the countryside into the metropolitan whirlpool can be expected only from regional planning, from a mutual adaptation of city and region, and from a coordinated transformation of the urban and rural areas in which the level of organic redevelopment would simultaneously rise as in communicating pipes. This does not mean a ruralization of urban areas or an urbanization of rural areas, but a leveling-up of both to a higher standard of cultural and material evolution and a reinstatement of human values as the supreme arbiters of all our efforts to revitalize the environment.

In every age and in most countries of the world Ideal Cities have been designed, and in some cases, built. They enshrined the purest and highest aspirations and a vision of the future. Today, Ideal Cities can no longer fulfill this mission. While only a few generations ago the village and the small town were almost self-sufficient units, today the world is our unit of thinking and acting.

But it is not only the world that is shrinking. Every country is undergoing the same transformation. In other words, the scale of our actions is widening. Translated into the language of city planning, this means that we have to design plans for the Ideal Region and for a country as a whole. All our cities have developed on ground plans conceived for small towns. They belong to an era that was far removed from our age with its violent social and economic, scientific and technological changes. Hitherto our efforts to reshape the urban and rural environment have not been attuned to this disturbing outlook. Intense mental exertions and clear vision are needed to adapt our ideas to these new conditions.

The *Ideal Region* is the result of a far-reaching redistribution of settlement, industry, and population, and of a reshaping of the environment in such a manner that it can absorb the new millions and offer them a dignified and productive existence. This demands the preparation of large-scale and long-term plans for vast regions within which a new structure of settlement can systematically grow up, and every community can serve distinctive functions as an organic part of the whole. This is the program for the Ideal Region. Let us not forget that the Ideal Cities of the past were social fanfares expressing the conscience and the longing of their age. The Ideal Region should do the same for our time.

What is a region and what is the meaning of regional integration? As long as the relations between town and country were relatively simple, it was not too difficult to find a workable size for a region. So it was in medieval Europe and in China where the towns were centers of a hinterland one day's journey in distance to and from the town. It was similar too in the Colonial period of the United States, when Philadelphia was the largest city because its hinterland was then the largest with the most fertile farmland. Today these simple relations, and with them the easy fixation of a well-defined region, have ceased to exist. Modern means of transport make boundaries illusory and bind together regions that are actually separated.

Regionalism is the result of functional spacing within a certain area. It is a process of gradual growth from inside this area; but it stretches out beyond the regional sphere towards other regions, establishing manifold contacts with them. Regionalism is a unifying force coordinating all activities that make up the life of a region.

The following quotation from *American Regionalism* by Odum and Moore gives an excellent summary of the problems involved:

Of great significance in the culture economy of regionalism [is] the decentralisation of people, of culture, and of pathology [which] may be attained in the new frontiers of American life. . . . Yet again such decentralisation does not apply only to the metropolitan regions or the planned towns and communities round the great cities. It takes into account the whole phenomenon of the new mobility of people, the migrations to and from cities, it comprehends movements to and from farms, providing technical ways for the reintegration of agrarian culture. . . . It points to the development of new frontiers of . . . culture which may provide new centres of health and recreation, of opportunity or urban decentralisation where surplus wealth may be expended or normal culture develop. . . . In the second place the region differs from the mere locality or pure geographic area in that it is characterised not so much by boundary lines and actual limits, by extension from a centre, and by fringe or border margins which separate one area from another. A key attribute of the region is, therefore, that it must be a *constituent unit in an aggregate whole or totality.* Inherent in the *region* as opposed to the mere locality or the isolated section is the essence of unity of which it can exist as a part. . . . In this more vital sense urbanism or metropolitanism is not regionalism in so far as urban centres seek their own ends regardless of relationship to other great centres or in opposition to national or rural ends.

Regionalism, as the connecting link between national and local planning, has to play a decisive role in the process of decentralization and dispersal. Its factual expression is, as already mentioned, the regional structure of settlement as produced by functional spacing. Functional spacing leads to two different, though closely interdependent, results; it assigns certain functions to each individual community, thus giving it a special character, and it balances this distribution of functions among the individual settlements of the region.

Neither the size of a settlement nor the number of its inhabitants nor its distance from the next place can determine the functions it can exert. On the contrary, the functions determine the size, distance, and number. The idea is that settlements with the same functions, especially with the same central services, can be equally spaced from each other. A hierarchy of communities where each rank controls those below it would be the opposite of everything national and regional planning stands for. It would perpetuate the existing structure and prevent coordination of the individual communities and collaboration between them as equal partners in regional integration.

We must look at the region as a whole and lift as many services as possible onto a regional basis. This point of view would mean an equal distribution of some basic services among all settlements of the region. It would also alter the relationship of some other functions, and it would provide a flexible framework for the complicated interblending of the numerous expressions and needs of modern life.

Regional integration embraces the *whole* life of a region. Social forces are the prime movers of the process. Economic factors are the buttresses giving them stability and guaranteeing their smooth working. Social and economic activities must be conceived and pursued on a regional basis, balancing local interests and rivalries.

In the social sphere an elastic framework of social services reaching every community and every citizen on an equal level must be developed, so that home life, recreation, social intercourse, and cultural activities find ever-widening opportunities and increasing stimulation. In the economic sphere a similar framework must be devised for the provision of work and the distribution of goods and all material amenities over a network of public utility services, bringing scientific and technological innovations within easy reach of every inhabitant of the region. This is, of course, only a rough classification of the manifold factors involved, but it will show the need for integration on a regional level.

Regional integration means the equal distribution of cultural and material goods over the whole region. It produces a regional association of all communities within a given area, rivaling each other in quality but not in quantity. It is, as it were, a neighborhood unit on a regional scale, which focuses the interests of its inhabitants on a common task and on a common purpose without reducing them to the narrow dullness of parochialism.

Regional integration demands:

1. Planning from the top and the bottom at the same time.

2. Organic growth from within.

3. Unity of rural and urban districts in the cultural, social, and economic sphere.

4. Interregional balance of internally homogeneous regions.

Planning from Top and Bottom. What is meant by planning from the top and the bottom at the same time? If we attempted to plan a region from the top, delimiting its size, redistributing its population and industry, developing a green grid, assessing its main activities, and allocating them among the different districts and localities within it, without taking into account the approach from the bottom, the local conditions and characteristics, we would create something like an empty shell.

At best the result would be a rigid framework within which the individual communities would lack functional interdependence and a balanced socio-economic structure. In other words, we must apply both the deductive and the inductive method, the former starting from the configuration as a whole and the latter leading from the particular to the general.

The approach from the top means that we must envisage a region as one functional unit and that every community within this unit may become a regional center for a particular purpose. In terms of physical and social planning, this approach implies physical and cultural decentralization and dispersal, resulting in a functional interrelationship between the community units.

There should, however, be no mistake; the physical environment this adaptation to new conditions creates is merely a means, not an end in itself. It is the physical framework within which every human activity can be carried on and every individual and social need can be fulfilled with the highest degree of efficiency. The regional plan should assign size, status, and function to the individual communities, replacing their subordination to the absorbing influence of the big cities and their sometimes overspecialized structure with a vigorous coordination and diversity.

Planning from the top consists, therefore, of a twofold approach. First, it is a diagnosis of the special character of the region as a whole and of the forces that make up the functional network of the region. Secondly, it is a modification of the existing pattern and a bringing-out of the inherent potentialities in the interaction all over the region.

Consequently, planning a region from the top is not a mere redistribution of what exists, but an eminently formative task, initiating a greater productivity and a rational adaptation of the natural resources to man's needs.

A simple example may be helpful. If we move to a new house, the first thing we do is adapt it in general to our personal taste and convenience. We brood over the best use of the different rooms; each should fulfill its purpose efficiently, and all together should form an integrated dwelling unit. The use of a number of rooms has been fixed from the very beginning; they correspond, as it were, to the natural resources of the region, such as coal, water, and fertile agricultural areas. Here we will build up our "fixed industries," cooking, washing, storing, and so on. The main issue with which we are confronted is how we intend to arrange our life.

These and similar considerations will be foremost in our mind before we settle down to furnish the individual rooms—the different "communities" of the house. To follow up the simile of the "region," both approaches—the approach from the top, the adaptation of the house to our needs and aspirations in general, and the approach from the bottom, the practical and attractive furnishing of the rooms—are interlocked, and we must think of both at the same time. And in each respect we are concerned first of all with bringing out the best qualities and developing the potentialities latent in the house and in each room.

The approach from the bottom—the furnishing of the rooms—is, in the main, an allocation of functions to the individual communities and districts of the region. We must know what every place and every district can offer under the existing conditions and what potential development promises the highest cultural and material returns. We must avoid a lopsided or a self-contained structure of communities and districts. However, it is not sufficient that every community and every district—urban and rural—produces what is best suited to it. It is essential that every activity can be carried on with the highest efficiency and that it is conceived as part and parcel of the regional scheme.

Organic Growth. Organic growth from within means the development of the constituent parts of the body, in this case the region, to their fullest capacity, by the provision of the right vitamins as a natural source of energy in the form most rapidly absorbed and used by the body. Vitamins are, in this connection, the right quality and the right quantity of social and economic services, which widen the opportunity of every community and district and of every citizen for a continuous expansion in the production and the use of goods and result in a rising standard of living for the *whole* population.

No body can grow without exercise, and no mind can develop without intellectual adventure. Both need, therefore, the appropriate tasks. These tasks can be provided in the form of work, recreation, and social intercourse. But favorable results can be expected only if every part of the "body" region is balanced to all the others and not impeded in its working. To achieve this goal, it is necessary to eliminate waste of resources, of time and space, and—to follow up the comparison—to eliminate all substances that have produced regional and local arteriosclerosis and to increase the efficiency of services and the scope of consumption and life in general.

Unity of Urban and Rural Districts.   As for the unity of rural and urban districts in the cultural, social, and economic sphere, we can restrict our comments to four principles.

Regional integration is the result of unity by diversity but not of uniformity by repetition. Unity by diversity means that the inhabitants of the region have a diverse opportunity in the choice of their occupation, their living places, and their recreational possibilities. Industrial and agricultural activities must be soundly balanced within the region as a whole, and within every district and every community there should be a sufficient number of different industries to make a lop-sided development of the labor market impossible. In general, unity by diversity will put the interdependence of all communities on a new basis if all cultural, social, and economic services and opportunities are accessible on the same level of quality and quantity to the whole population.

A regional scheme must embrace the whole region without any discrimination between rural and urban districts. It is an indivisible plan in a spatial sense just as much as in a structural sense. Let me quote in this connection a passage from Mumford's *The Culture of Cities*. It gives the essence of the problem we have to solve.

Plans must result in a more complicated pattern and a more comprehensive life for the region, for this geographic area can only now, for the first time, be treated as an instantaneous whole for all functions of social existence. Instead of trusting to the mere massing of population to produce the necessary social concentration and social drama, we must now seek these results through deliberate community planning and closer regional linkages. One might call this new method of designing city and region in working partnership the principle of unity by apportioned distribution rather than unity by centralisation. The latter means physical spreading and control from a dominant centre, whereas the first means functional spotting. Any one part of such a complex may become, for a special purpose, the centre of the region.

Interregional Balance.   Regional integration does not stop at the boundries of the individual regions. It makes provision for interregional cooperation. Consequently, a regional scheme must take into account not only the forces working within the region but also those of other regions. The former have the tendency to move outward, while the latter exert their influence inward upon the region.

It is comparable to a railway station: its layout in general and its technical installations in detail handle the outgoing and incoming trains. The internal structure depends not only on the number of passengers and the quantity of goods arriving in this particular place but also on the impact of the traffic along the whole length of all the lines converging on it. The station building itself is a clearly delimited entity, but around it spreads the web of the railway tracks and the marshaling yards, interspersed with numerous sheds and other constructions, forming a marginal area.

The same holds good for a region except that for administrative reasons its exact delimitation defies precision. Its actual boundaries are marginal areas, but not dotted lines like those on maps. These areas are traversed by long filaments thrust out from any population center within the region to other centers far away in other parts of the country.

The main conclusion that should be drawn from the foregoing definition of regional planning is that it does not stop outside the boundaries of urban areas. The Ideal Region comprises both rural and urban areas, including what was previously the metropolis or the big regional city. The ideal and functional preponderance of urban agglomerations has disappeared. Their activities and social and cultural attractions have been distributed among the new regional community units.

The new environmental structure will need several generations to materialize, but the groundwork should be laid and the direction in which our efforts are to move should be charted now. This is the minimum we can do if we expect posterity to look back at our time not with a feeling of despair and contempt but with pride and gratitude for the insight and vision of our own generation.

In the course of this work I have repeatedly warned of the realism of the so-called realists and of the planners for chaos. I have to repeat this warning, for in the short period since the first hesitant steps toward regional planning experience has already taught us that these groups of pseudo-planners will do all in their power to oppose and to thwart this development. They are the same people who believe that they are "modern" and "progressive," when they fill their homes with labor- and money-saving gadgets. They are the same zealots who hope to imprison the spirit of the future in the mold of outworn social ideals. Their self-deceptions make them blind to the profound changes that are going on in the mind of humanity as a whole. They fail to see that even words are changing their meaning—that ideas take on a totally different sense and that their implications are far removed from what they have been in the past.

This revolution of the mind that is spreading all over the world is tantamount to a crisis of consciousness. This crisis is the most potent force demanding a transformation of our environment, on a scale and with an intensity that has not occurred in previous eras. What distinguishes it even from the agricultural and urban revolutions is that we are more conscious—or that we are at least more able to be conscious

—of the changes we initiate ourselves and that we can make these changes deliberately and, if we want, systematically.

I admit that the picture is not too bright, if we look at the world stage, especially at the political scene, where the human drama is enacted. The Cold War is perhaps the most telling example. It is fought with slogans, with prestige values, and with the obsolete weapons of power politics, not with ideas, human values, or the clarity and integrity of purpose that alone can release the creative faculties of groups and individuals. Like many other spheres of life, city planning has been a victim of this unfortunate attitude.

And yet we should try to rid ourselves of the comforting but dangerous escape into a world of double standards: one for Sundays, brimming over with shallow and pious intentions and a consummate conciliation of personal interests and vague public ideals, and one for weekdays, full of so-called realistic and pragmatic tinkering with details. There is but one standard that should dominate all our thoughts and actions. The standard of the highest morality and of the highest human values should be our only yardstick. We are still far removed from this goal, but we should exert all our efforts to follow the road that leads in this direction.

The creation of a physical environment for the masses and for the individuals who compose the masses is a step in this direction. The dynamic equilibrium between the whole and the parts has been submerged in our subconscious. It has to be restored, to be brought to the surface—but without surface values. There is now much talk going on about functional design, but where is the harmony of functional and social forces in the reformation of our environment? It does not exist—not yet.

Some people, the image-chasers, hope to resuscitate the image of the city by making it "legible." Why do they not try to create the image of a region? Are they too timid to adapt their ideas to the expanding scale, expanding in scope and diversity? Whence this mental timidity? We need a greater flexibility of mind and a new vision and, above all, to use Mirabeau's famous exhortation: *De l'audace! Encore de l'audace! Toujours de l'audace!*

Regional planning, if rightly understood, demands this ever-present audacity. It will encounter great obstruction and difficulties. But so does the conquest of space. Why should we not be genuine realists? Why not employ the same energy, the same inventiveness, and all our means to this terrestrial adventure and adapt our environment, before we land a man on the moon, to the challenge of the new world that is emerging, in which generations to come must live?

National Planning

Just like local and regional planning, regional and national planning overlap. National planning is primarily concerned with the working out of principles, not with detailed investigations or with the working out of comprehensive plans. Regional and national planning have gained recognition in Europe and parts of Asia as indispensable instruments for improving the environment. In this country there still exists a widespread distrust of everything concerned with planning. The climate is not too propitious, and it may be doubtful whether anything beyond local planning will ever be fully utilized. What are the essential problems that are the proper domain of national and interregional planning? Are these problems really so antagonistic to the present trend, and are they so new that the distrust is justified?

Regional planning, and for that matter "national" planning, have existed in antiquity, in the Greek city-states and in Roman times, as urban-rural integration of large areas. In the Middle Ages the urban region included towns and their surrounding countryside. This dynamic interaction began to dissolve when industrial development disintegrated the physical and social structure of settlement and finally broke down the clearly defined boundaries of the urban sphere of influence.

Today the problems are greater, but the task has remained the same: to restore a sound balance between city and country and between regions. Living space for the new millions has to be provided. Nobody will deny that it is impossible to accommodate the population increase in the existing urban conglomerations, even if they are improved by city renewal, which in any case would not appreciably increase the dwelling space but rather reduce it, if renewal means a loosening-up of the urban area. Consequently, one of the main tasks of national planning is sorting out regions as reception or evacuation areas for the growing population. This should be done only by a very general apportionment, but the main trends of a redistribution of population and industry should be defined.

Other tasks that have already been undertaken and solved with considerable success in the United States are the preservation of national parks, the mobilization of water and other resources, and the building of a grid of interstate highways. All this involves not only physical but also economic planning and far-reaching sociological investigations and a national land-use policy.

In general, national planning should provide a guidance system that is flexible enough to serve as the basis for future plans and decisions going beyond local and purely regional interests and to balance conflicting pressures which inevitably emanate from too parochial an attitude among competing communities and regions. The mere concentration of population in a given area will never contribute anything to social awareness and collective creativity, the essential prerequisites of a community spirit and a fertile dramatization of social life.

After all that has been explained on the foregoing pages there is no need to enter into a detailed description of what national planning should be. I have done this in my *Creative Demobilization*. But we may summarize the main lines of action which are instrumental in the planning of new settlements and in the reshaping of those already existing. They are:

1. The articulation of large regions, through a system of *linear arteries* forming the primary grid of parks, parkways, and highways, to serve the functional needs of recreation and circulation.

2. The differentiation of the apportioned living space, through a system of *spatial zoning* organizing the available land into residential and nonresidential areas, to serve the functional needs of housing and working.

3. The subdivision of these areas through a system of *functional spotting*, providing the secondary grid of open spaces and roads, to serve the functional needs of the local units, their internal structure, layout, and interconnected groupings.

All these three methods should be combined and applied simultaneously and systematically over vast regions.

They are the fundamentals of local, regional, and national planning and, if wisely used, can inaugurate an era of a creative revolution of environment.

Whatever the defenders of a "flexible *status quo*" may say, the twilight of cities is a fact, and the imperative need to provide sufficient and stimulating living space for the new millions is also a fact. We have the means to harmonize these two truths and to make them the cornerstones of the transformation of our urban and rural environment on a large scale. We can do it—but only if we will it, and attune our vision to the future.

chapter four

THE FOURTH

DIMENSION

"From henceforth space by itself and
time by itself are doomed to fade away
into mere shadows and only a kind of union
of the two will preserve an independent
reality."—MINKOWSKI

The discovery of the third dimension, in this case
the concentration of ever more people or offices in ever
higher buildings, has been hailed as a major contribution to
city planning. It has gained a wide currency, especially
among the younger architects and city planners; but this is
no proof that it can arrest the social or even the physical
deterioration of our cities. Only within a much larger framework can this method be useful. In the narrow and congested
urban areas it merely adds to the overcrowding and prevents
the emergence of a new social awareness and a new *élan
vital*. We have to go a step further. We have to discover the
realistic interpretation of the fourth dimension, of the unity
of time and space, and to make this unity the basis of local,
regional, and national renewal.

THE NEW SCALE

Ever since man first gave thought to his place in the universe, the scale that determined his observations and his concept of space has been widening, and his existence and his ideas have been related in some way or other to centers fixed in time and space. Our generation stands at the turning point of this long line of development, a turning point that Giordano Bruno's vision of a universe, infinite in time and space, had anticipated. His thought was so great and bold that it has never ceased to grip the imagination. It is an experience that has affected everybody, that has upset the innocent mind of every child: the old cozy idea of the celestial vault that covered the world like a bowl goes to pieces, and the subconscious and still confused vision of infinite space dawns upon us.

Now we have to reconcile two diametrical opposites: the infinitely great and the infinitely small. We have to find our way through a seemingly unsystematic and incoherent mass of phenomena and ideas. The new scale means not merely an expansion but also a limitation in space and time. How does this new polarity affect the concept that underlines and directs the transformation of the physical structure of environment? When we ask this question, we should be aware that in every period man's ideas of space and scale were concordant, whether he applied them to the universe or to his own terrestrial world.

The smallest unit is the community. Its size is limited by social cohesion. Its location is determined by the concurrence of all the essential factors that guarantee the maximum effect of the social program. Neither size nor location should be dependent, in the first instance, on economic considerations. Only where there are absolutely unavoidable considerations, such as in the case of fixed industries such as mining or ports, economic factors may take first place. In all other circumstances they must be subordinated to the full play of social forces.

At this point the realists will tell me that these demands amount to pure "insanity," that economic man must be sovereign, and that social man is merely a desirable by-product or that a "workable compromise" should be worked out. I do not deny them the right to their opinions, but I would remind them that their gospel of economic determinism and economic preponderance has created the chaotic conditions of our urban environment.

Let us make this point quite clear. The only "center" that has any real and creative significance is man as a human being, not as a working animal. As a human being he can be everywhere, and everywhere his personal life can exert a fruitful and consolidating influence without being fixed in time or space. He is a "mobile center" and it is around this center that the new concept of space and scale should revolve.

The social units of which these human centers are the constituent parts are the new communities distributed organically over the country, forming an integrated whole in which every unit stands in functional relationship to others, without the domineering preponderance of a "happy few" big cities to the disadvantage of all the others. On the face of it, this redistribution of settlement may seem not to differ essentially from the existing structure, provided that it has been loosened up to a certain degree and improved by some reforms. In reality it is quite different in essence and appearance. It marks the end of satellite towns and suburbs, and restores a productive balance between equally or almost equally important communities.

The largest unit is comparable to a galaxy of stars, all more or less of the same order, dispersed over the country at intervals determined by the functional relationship among the community units but not by their distance from a central city. In the past the intervals between units of settlement increased in proportion to their distance from the urban center: the greater the power of attraction of the center, the more numerous and closer together were the smaller units of settlement. Instead of one galaxy for the whole country, we had—and still have—quite a number of planets, each a big city, and each planet, with all its satellites—the towns and small places—revolving around the sun—the capital city and metropolis.

If the Everyman family lives in a place two hours' journey from where was once upon a time the great metropolis, they will not have the weekly problem of whether "to go to town" or not. They will find that everything that attracted their grandparents to the city is now within easy reach. Cultural goods, social amenities, and economic facilities have become mobile or have been so distributed and split up that every community has a direct or indirect share in them. The thoughts of the family no longer move along a one-way street toward the great city, alluring like a lost paradise and overbearing like rich relations. They turn around in all directions because every community has become the seat of some cultural and social activities of a higher order.

The Everymans may feel like Anatole France's dog Riquet, whose reactions are described in *Pensées de Ricquet* in *Crainquebille: "Les hommes, les animaux, les pierres grandissent en s'approchant et deviennent enormes quand ils sont sur moi. Moi non. Je demeure toujours aussi grand, partout où je suis."* In other words, the Everymans will be free from the provincial inferiority complex and yet modest enough to understand that their own community is but one among equals.

And this is perhaps the main change, for the new scale is the composite result of two heterogeneous processes: of a dispersal of cities and towns and their shrinking into the small units of organic communities and, at the same time, of an expanding living space. It is something similar to what Sir Arthur Eddington describes in *The Expanding Universe:*

If this lecture room were to expand to twice its present size, the seats all separating from each other in proportion, you would notice that everyone had moved away from you. . . . It is not you they are avoiding; everyone is having the same experience. . . . It is a general scattering apart, having no particular centre of dispersal.

This new concept of "a general scattering apart" will find its embodiment in the future structure of settlement, just as the heliocentric universe of Copernicus, and before it, the geocentric universe of Aristotle were reflected in the layout of contemporary cities and towns. There will be no central cities, no conurbations, no absorbing spheres of influence to disturb the balance of functional interdependence between the numerous community units. Loosely grouped industrial units will be located at larger intervals.

The new scale has been defined above as a union between expansion and limitation. In terms of physical planning, this means that the numerous small communities are to be made organic entities within the wide and flexible framework of regional unity. As formative components of this spatial pattern, the community units exert a double influence: they are like pylons carrying the regional linkages of cultural and functional integration, and at the same time they are the social substructure on which the ever-changing human drama is acted.

The interaction between the communities and the region is a process of growth and transformation with its own particular scale and equilibrium. The scale of the over-all picture widens, while the scale of the constituent parts shrinks. The new region is a functional collective held together by the cooperation of the communities and by regional homogeneity in all social and cultural matters.

To conceive physical planning, be it on a local or regional level, in terms of agriculture, industry, city, town, and village, or even in those of farmers or peasants, industrial workers or employees in offices, is an anomaly, a remnant of the past with its reliance on institutional details. We should conceive physical planning by thinking in processes instead of in institutions, thus bringing out the potential development of the regional collective as a whole and relating every individual objective to the configuration in its entirety.

Regional delimitations are mostly artificial and impede an organic development. They further parochialism and stand in the way of a genuine unity of life. The confrontation with the irreducible diversity of existence cannot be fully experienced within the limits of fictitious parochial loyalties that diminish the awareness of events beyond the narrow circle of ordinary life. The new scale is more than a novel aspect of our physical environment. It is an intellectual adventure into the totality of the circumstances that surround us. It releases direct and indirect sensations, reactions to what we can see immediately around us, and reactions to what we can sense by an association of ideas of the wider environment and what we can explore in our mind.

THE NEW
MOBILITY

The welding together of time and space creates a new mobility. Although we cannot conceive the fourth dimension with anything like the same clarity as the third, it is a revelation we can believe in—the more readily because our practical experience tells us that distances are relative and that mobility of body and mind is as essential to our existence as the circulation of blood. The discovery of the fourth dimension has created a new attitude, an awakening to the immense possibilities that life without ideal and material boundaries and, in this particular connection, without the overpowering attraction of the big urban centers, holds in store. It means the free and easy mobility of men and of material and immaterial goods.

The new mobility is a special sort of mobility, or rather a state of mind: less thought is given to the actual location of the places between which men and goods have to travel than to the time needed to cover the distances between the places where cultural and social activities or economic facilities are offered. The new mobility contains all the elements needed to make man feel that he is irrevocably related to the general scheme of things as an individual and social being.

The whole "culture space" is his living place, and the

intricately interwoven combination of all functions, the whole plexus of all contributions from all community units creates that unity in diversity and that sensibility to values that alone can lift life above the level of Being to that of Becoming. It is a change that is similar to the contrast between thinking in static concepts and thinking in processes.

Our present situation has something in common with the "Theory of Ghosts" to which Eddington refers in *The Expanding Universe:*

In a perfectly spherical world rays of light emitted in all directions from a point will, after travelling round the world, converge to the same point; thus a real image is formed from which light will again diverge in all directions. Such an image might optically be mistaken for a substantial body.

The space would then be populated not only with real stars but with ghosts of stars that existed thousands of millions of years ago. The ghosts would be ". . . formed at the place occupied by the star when the light was emitted . . . the star may have since been scattered into many fragments." The ghosts are the old urban centers, still emitting light but being unreal. The new "fragments" are the new small community centers. Unfortunately, however, there are still many people who are taken in by the light which the ghost cities emit.

The pull of dispersal spreads significant life over a wider area, and through this "fragmentation" it releases forces that could not mature within the narrow circle of urban existence. The new mobility creates conditions which are far removed from the cumbersome journey to work or the difficulties of social intercourse in our present cities. They are in striking contrast to life in the Middle Ages and antiquity, when living and working place, office, storeroom, and sales-room were mostly under the same roof, when social events were almost wholly restricted to one's own town, and fairs were still the meeting places of men and goods.

Our mobility has increased in proportion to the increase in scale: from the pedestrian scale it grew into the carriage scale, then the railway scale, into the motor car scale and the fast traffic along superhighways, and finally into the scale of the airplane and rockets. The effect of this increase in scale upon the mobility we could enjoy today is still very sporadic. We still think of the structure of settlement as a multitude of fixed points, not as a network of distances, and even far less as a ratio of extensions; but it is precisely this last concept that, according to Eddington, alone has a "physical reality."

Length is relative. The average journey between home and work or any other place of cultural or social activity in a big city takes about one hour from door to door. If the obstacles inevitably connected with urban concentration did not exist and the new living space covered a wide area within which fast traffic could move without restrictions and delays, we could expect to cover 50 to 60 miles in one hour. Or, in not too distant a future, 100 to 150 miles on electrically controlled highways. In an area with a radius of this length, a considerable number of community units could easily be located. We would then apply a standard of comparison different from that we have been used to.

What is meant by this standard may be easier to understand if we revert once more to Eddington's definition of the relativity of length that he gives in *The Expanding Universe:*

Reckoning of length always implies comparison with a standard of length, so that length is relative to a comparison standard. It is only the ratio of extensions that enters into experience. Suppose that every length in the universe were doubled; nothing in our experience would be altered. We cannot even attach a meaning to the supposed change. It is an empty form of words—as though an international conference should decree that the pound should henceforth be reckoned two pounds, the dollar two dollars, the mark two marks, and so on.

The new structure of settlement will develop by exactly the same process; by a general moving apart without maintaining particular centers of dispersal, namely, cities. It is a transformation that affects equally all parts of the former structure: the distances have increased everywhere, not only between a few places. Our standard of judgment has changed correspondingly. Nothing has happened. The main obstacles to change are always in our mind. If the possibility of comparison with the old standards has disappeared, the new mobility cannot be an experience we should distrust or try to avoid.

The new mobility has been characterized as a new attitude, as a breaking away from a life within narrow circles focused on urban centers. It is an emotional and intellectual liberation. It will demonstrate that creative energies can be fully released in small communities absorbing the dualism between externals and fundamentals, between the façade of life and its essence. It is a process that derives its power of development not from abstractions but from living entities, incessantly in a process of creation and change, and confronts us with a paradoxical situation.

The theory of evolution implies an ever-increasing degree of organization of life, while thermodynamics denotes a decreasing degree of orderliness of the universe. In our particular case we have, on the one hand, the increasing organization of society and of life in general, and on the other, the decreasing intelligibility of the interaction of the innumerable details which make up the totality of existence. If physicists say that the universe is gradually "running down" because of an increase of disorder, they mean in reality a greater complexity, a more complicated pattern of manifoldness.

The new small community units create such a host of novel problems, such a complex "disorder" that it seems to burst the habitual order of life. But this is merely our first reaction, before the new "disorder" has seeped down to the level of common-sense acceptance, and before the new pattern of living has become part and parcel of the next stage of development in the organization of society.

The new mobility creates "disorder" by revealing unexpected aspects and potentialities and by producing a simultaneity in space and time that we have not been used to before. We are in general more inclined to accept changes if they affect only the details of life, but we are very obstructive if they threaten to disrupt the intricate web of the totality of our existence.

The new mobility, the fourth dimension, or space-time —all these terms express in this context "thinking in processes," seeing the relationships between details and the whole, and acting in accordance with this insight. It means, therefore, the transfer of energies, hitherto concentrated in the cities and unable to develop freely, to small communities, and their integration with the social and economic structure in all its manifestations. Compared with the past, this thinking and living in processes has the same differentiating qualities that distinguish a Renaissance painting, with its fixed perspective, from one by Picasso, with its plural views, rendering objects transparent and mobile.

If we can consider every place within the expanding environment as an integral part of the cultural and social scene in which we are the actors, the stratification of communities and functions disappears. Any place may make an outstanding contribution in any particular field, but none will exert a dominant influence, making it a center of physical and functional concentration.

The former classification of urban communities as commercial, industrial, mining, port cities, and so on becomes meaningless. Their functions have been split up among the new communities and the industrial units interspersed between them. These ideas, which may seem "unrealistic," are in keeping with the conceptions underlying the revolutionary transformation in science and art, in technology, and in the relationship of national states in a rapidly shrinking world.

Those who are concerned with the transformation of the physical environment cannot stand aside. They should not be afraid to demolish cherished illusions and to explore what is and what could be, not what we are used to or what suits us at the moment. The realists, whom I have already repeatedly criticized in this work, will ridicule these ideas and denounce them as "fantastic"; but since I am not concerned with city officials or city planners but with city planning and the "physical reality" of life, I cannot avoid repeating once more that their influence is still a grave obstacle to progress. Their advice has not been too helpful in the past. They are responsible not only for the chaotic conditions of our cities but also for most of the major disasters that their *Realpolitik* has inflicted on mankind.

Their standards of judgment and their scale of comparison are at fault. They seem to be willing to forget that the scale of destruction has widened and that all the precious investments in dead things, in buildings, utilities, and other services, will be lost in the next conflagration, which is inevitable if their influence continues and if they persist in diverting valuable energies and means from internal reconstruction to the external adventure of war.

It is, however, rather awkward that the next war may be more harmless than we can hope. The neutron bomb would not be a blessing to progressive city planners. It would kill millions of people and leave the material achievements of our civilization intact. It would not, like the old-fashioned bombs of the last war, raze whole districts to the ground and thus create great opportunities for a constructive renewal. It would save all cities and all the costly investments, and, if some of the realists should survive, they could start again where they left off.

The power of these *Realpolitiker*—there are *Realpolitiker* in all spheres of life, not excluding physical planning—is greater than most people dare to believe. They challenge our credulity and complacent conformity. But a challenge is something to be taken up, not something that can be used as an excuse for evading the real issues and doing nothing.

Let me repeat and apply to our problem the words in which C. P. Snow expressed the imperative need for nuclear disarmament when he addressed the meeting of the American Association for the Advancement of Science in 1960: "I am saying this as responsibly as I can. On the one side we have a finite risk. On the other side we have a certainty of disaster. Between a risk and a certainty a sane man does not hesitate." The peaceful revolution of environment involves certain risks. But these risks have to be faced, and the problems connected with these risks have to be solved. They can be solved, if we understand the impelling moral nature of the challenge and act accordingly.

chapter five

PROGRAM

OF ACTION

THE twilight now descending upon towns, cities, and metropolises marks the end of a perennial revolution that has shaped and reshaped urban communities all over the world for more than five thousand years. The problems that have accumulated during these millennia, bringing about the present crisis, are manifold, and their interaction is complex and far-reaching.

The Problems. An understanding of the potentialities in the situation is of primary importance. If we are to evade the disastrous consequences of this development and find a way out of the impasse, we must turn the apathy of the public into constructive cooperation.

195

This is the first problem to be solved before a Revolution of Environment on a large scale can be initiated. An educational program is needed to dispel the fog of complacent credulity, misunderstanding, and illusion that shrouds the true nature of the problems.

Some of the most pressing problems that demand clarification as the starting points of future action are summarized in the following questions:

Why are cities surrounded by the invisible walls of constricting administrative boundaries, by the girdles of local taxation, and the parochial urban mentality, leading to mutual frustration and selfish rivalry between neighboring communities?

Why are cities regarded as the sole and supreme potential agents of economic, social, and cultural progress, and as the unalterable mode of community life?

Why are uncontrolled growth, urban chaos and sprawl, blight and obsolescence, congestion, air pollution and noise accepted as unavoidable by-products of city life?

Why have urban nomadism and the illusion of social and cultural proximity submerged the personal life of urbanites and suburbanites in a welter of ever-growing demands of the working life?

Why do people acquiesce in the doubtful blessings of a Synthetic City, with its artificial provision of trivial, commercialized, and pseudocultural amenities, with its Cult of Bigness and its impersonal and predominantly utilitarian attitude to man and environment?

Why has the Cult of the Street, the still revered gospel of city planners that has lasted for more than five centuries, led to ever greater congestions of the urban areas instead of resulting in an easy flow of traffic?

Why has the lopsided partnership between urban and rural areas reduced the countryside to an appendix of the cities, useful only for weekend excursions or as a source of food supply?

Why are science and technology only halfheartedly employed in city planning and architecture, continuing and aggravating misdirected trends?

Why is the effect of progressing automation upon working hours and jobs allowed to result in increasing unemployment instead of in creative personal re-education?

Why is the population explosion that threatens all countries of the world expected to be absorbed by the antiquated existing urban conglomerations?

These are some, though by no means all, of the problems that have to be solved in a spirit of realistic audacity, breaking through the thought barrier and turning away the expediency mentality of narrow *Realpolitiker*.

The Objectives.   The present situation is the terminal constellation from which the potential development has to start.

The over-all objective is the creation of an inspiring and diversified environment and the release of environmental forces that generate a dynamic equilibrium among all parts of a country.

The splitting up of the amorphous mass of urban conglomerates into small, meaningful, and imaginable units restores a personal attitude toward the environment, revitalizing the countryside and raising it to the same cultural level as the urban areas.

Previously underdeveloped or overcrowded metropolitan regions are opened up or thinned out, offering new living space for the existing and new millions that have to be accommodated during the next decades.

The result of a systematic dispersal and relocation of settlement and population, industry and cultural opportunities, is the Ideal Region. This means the end of urban chaos and sprawl and their detrimental effect upon human values and aspirations, and the end of the domination of society by individual interests.

Genuine social and cultural proximity is one of the main characteristics of the Ideal Region, and easy mobility makes every place equally accessible without cumbersome delays, widening the mental outlook and the choice of opportunities.

Organic limitations of individual communities, interconnected by a grid of continuous parks, parkways, and highways, reduce traveling even over long distances to a minimum in time.

Science and technology are applied with imagination and foresight for clearly defined ends, as servants of society, not as utilitarian playthings or tools for practical purposes but as potential generators of a liberated and creative attitude to life in its totality.

Leisure and recreation assume the constructive role of agents of personal creativity and harmonious images of the world around us, lifting our minds above indifferent perception to the level of direct and intimate experience of the phenomena of our environment.

The realization of these objectives makes the fulfillment of apparently incompatible requirements possible in an environmental structure that combines and offers:

Compactness and openness of settlement
Order and flexibility
Differentiation and homogeneity
Privacy and social intercourse

The Methods. The procedure in *general* demands the integration of local, regional, and national planning in time and space through a systematic redistribution of population, settlement, and industry, and a dispersal of the urban congested areas. This process creates a flexible framework within which the daily cycle of homelife, work, recreation, and circulation can proceed with the maximum efficiency at all levels of the replanned region.

The principle of communicating pipes is to be observed: for every portion of living space taken out from the congested areas a corresponding portion in the new communities has to be provided.

The procedure in *detail* evolves from small-scale to large-scale transformations.

1. No slum areas are to be rebuilt. They are to be retained as open spaces or playgrounds, however small they may be.

2. A central open space is to be developed by a gradual thinning out of the core area in every city.

3. Only the absolutely essential functions of administration and commerce are to be concentrated in a small but loosely laid out *Desk City* at the fringes of the central open space.

4. A continuous grid of parks, parkways, and highways for superspeed travel is to be developed, covering

the whole country. All traffic arteries are to be made part of the natural landscape.

5. New community units, restricted in size and functions, are to be remapped and laid out, and new regions are to be opened up.

6. Industrial units are to be dispersed at suitable intervals between the residential communities.

7. The character of the streets is changed from the uniform nondescript canyon to open ribbons, rhythmically articulated by buildings and natural features with free views to other parts of the communities.

8. Cultural and social facilities are organically distributed among the community units, and cultural opportunities, as far as possible, are made mobile.

These are the main methods for initiating and sustaining a revolution of environment on a large scale. It is a task that will occupy the energy and the resources of several generations. It is obvious that no blueprint for the exact procedure to be followed can be worked out, but what we should do now is indicate the direction in which we must move, and begin laying the foundations for the next stage of development. In a shrinking world distances are increasingly meaningless. This is perhaps the greatest change to which we have to attune our thinking and acting, our plans for the Ideal Region of the future, within which every community can fulfill its functions unimpeded by the traditional ballast that has piled up over centuries.

This Program of Action can become a reality, if we will it and devote our whole personality to this adventure into a world which we create ourselves. Let me conclude with the words of two men, a philosopher and a poet, an American and a Russian. Their voices resound in a unison of particular strength and actuality.

In *A Week on the Concord and Merrimack Rivers* Henry Thoreau expressed the hope that although

history accumulates like rubbish before the portals of Nature, there is only necessary a moment's vanity and sound senses, to teach us that there is a nature behind the ordinary, in which we have only some vague preemption right. . . . We live on the outskirts of that region.

And Boris Pasternak's exhortation:

> "And never, for a single moment,
> Betray your credo or pretend,
> But be alive—this only matters,
> Alive and burning, to the end."

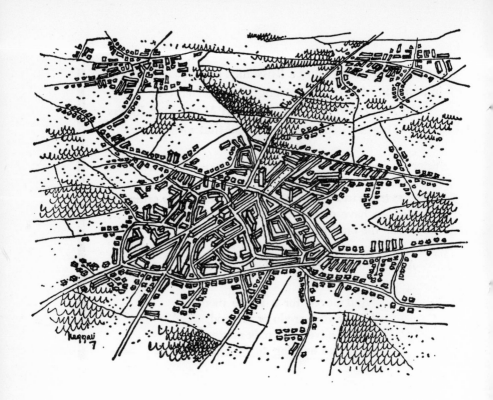

Antagonism of town and country
Landscape tolerated
Imperfect decentralization
Hierarchy of localities
The monster with tentacles
Social stratification
Cultural concentration
Industrial disorder
Rural isolation
Archaic farming units
Production commands

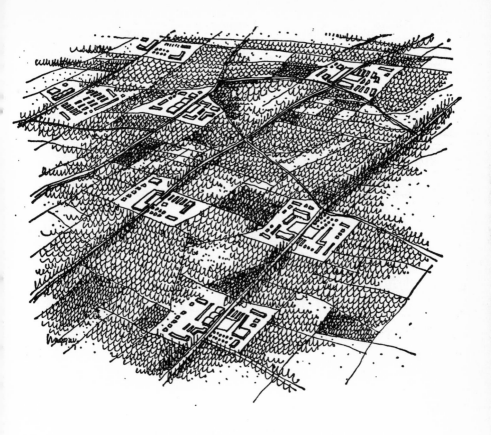

One living area
Landscape omnipresent
Perfect dispersal
Equality of communities
The loose cluster
Social affinity
Cultural ubiquituousness
Industrial isolation
Rural integration
Rational farming units
Consumption demands

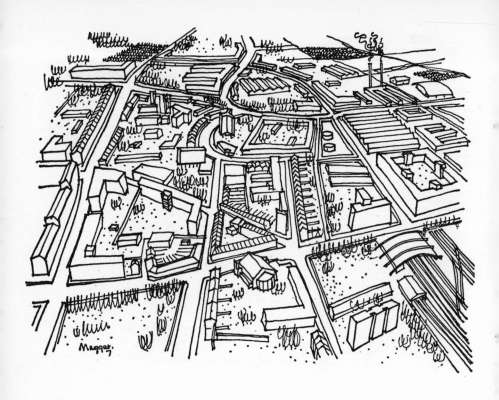

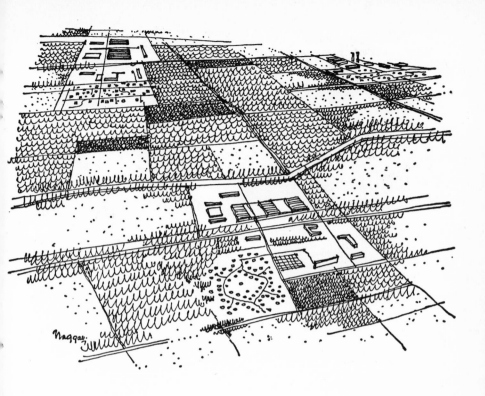

Small units
Expanding environment
Vitality and openness
Unity by diversity
The continuous park
Social centre
Re-creation
Social awareness
Industry and Agriculture
Culture: the whole environment

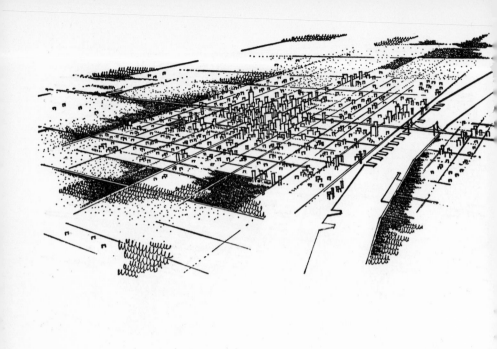

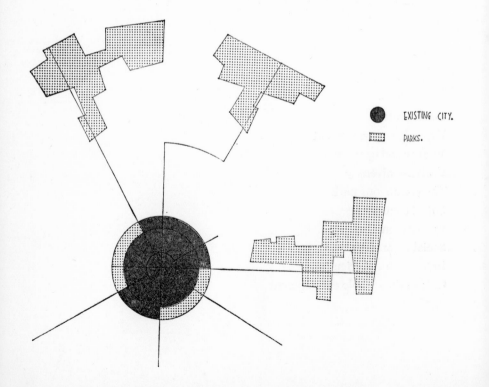

EXISTING CITY.

PARKS.

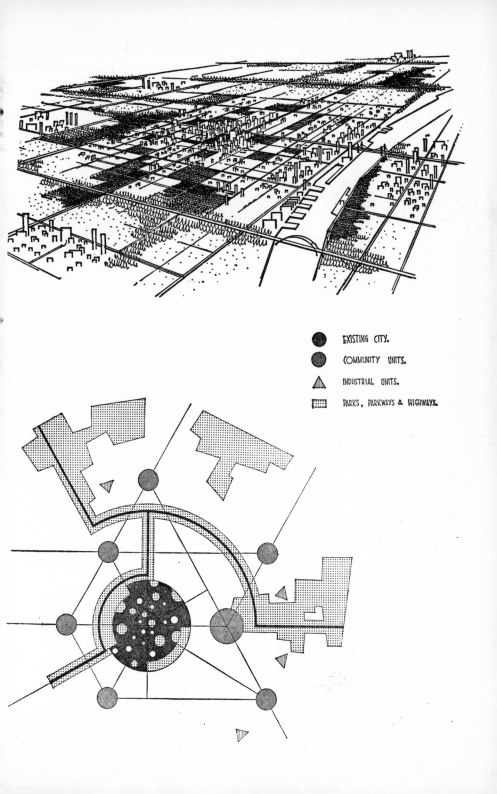

EXISTING CITY.

COMMUNITY UNITS.

INDUSTRIAL UNITS.

PARKS, PARKWAYS & HIGHWAYS.

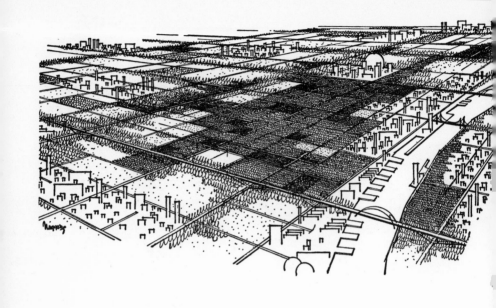

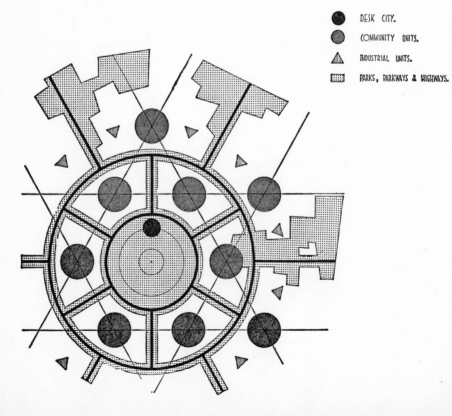

● DESK CITY.

● COMMUNITY UNITS.

▲ INDUSTRIAL UNITS.

▦ PARKS, PARKWAYS & HIGHWAYS.

Dickens 2-2356

DIDDE *Office Supply and Printing Inc.*
24 WEST SIXTH AVENUE • EMPORIA, KANSAS

Customer's
Order No._____ Date *12-13* 196*2*

M *Mrs F. L. Gilson*

Address_____

SOLD BY	CASH	C.O.D.	CHARGE	ON ACCT.	MDSE. RET.	PD. OUT	
D.			←				

QUAN.	DESCRIPTION	PRICE	AMOUNT
1	*Jumbo Paper mate refill*		79
		TAX	2
		TOTAL	81

ALL Claims and Returned Goods M U S T be accompanied by this bill.

0514

_____ Rec'd By_____

DIDDE OFFICE SUPPLY & PRTG. CO., EMPORIA, KANS.